Kirsty in the studio – 2003. (YFA)

KIRSTY

ANGEL OF COURAGE

The little girl who touches our hearts

Susie Mathis

Edited by Stephen Holby

Medavia

Medavia Publishing
An imprint of Boltneck Publications Limited
WestPoint, 78 Queens Road, Clifton, Bristol BS8 1QX

www.boltneck.com

This edition published by Medavia Publishing 2006
Second Impression 2006

A CIP catalogue of this book is available from the British Library

ISBN 0 9546399 5 2
ISBN 97809546399 5 2

Typeset in $10\frac{1}{2}$/12pt Palatino by
Academic and Technical Typesetting, Bristol
Printed and bound by The Bath Press

Cover design by Mark Ralph ATT & Clive Birch © 2006
Cover picture by *Manchester Evening News*

CONTENTS

Kirsty. (YFA)

For Kirsty with affection and pride

With special thanks to Louise Blenkharn, without whose expertise and patience this book would never have happened.

Through tears and laughter, I am indebted to dear Lou.

David kisses Kirsty at the Lowry Hotel, 2005. (CG MEN)

FOREWORD

by David Beckham OBE

Bravery and courage are words that are sometimes used too often and lightly. I know what true courage and real bravery are because I have seen them in a young girl who I am honoured and proud to count as a friend.

When I first met Kirsty Howard, I was blown away by her smile. In spite of all she is going through, there is always that glowing and warm smile.

I remember being really nervous before the World Cup qualifier against Greece. It was an important match, and we needed a result to get to the 2002 World Cup.

Kirsty, who was the mascot that day, was introduced to me before the game. She wasn't phased at all and was so calm. I was more nervous than her, but she put me at ease in an instant.

We have had many memorable moments together, from the Commonwealth Games to BBC Sports Personality of the Year, but she never ceases to amaze me with her strength and spirit. I have never met anyone like Kirsty and I doubt I ever will again.

Sister Aloysius with Kirsty. (HR)

PREFACE

by Sister Aloysius

In retrospect, looking back at the planning of Francis House, it was a natural development in the work of the Catholic Children's Rescue Society. From its origin in 1886 the Catholic Children's Society has cared for children, firstly within the large children's homes which later adapted to family group homes, adoption, fostering, family support, work with the deaf, physically disabled children and, as they were then known, Mother and Baby Homes.

In 1990 a new Social Worker, Jim Buggy, joined the Rescue staff. He highlighted the need in the area for children with a short life expectancy, a number of children he had discovered in his work with Manchester Social Services.

I have been privileged to work in the Children's Rescue Society since 1951, so have lived and worked through the many changes and served for a considerable number of years on the Rescue Council. In 1990, Father Tom Mulheran had been in charge of the Children's Society for 19 years. He was at all times open to hearing the needs of children and, on leaving the Children's Society to take on a diocesan post, also became Chaplain of Francis House Children's Hospice.

Along with Jim, I was asked to research the provisions already in existence and possible further needs, and to report back to each monthly Council Meeting. At that time the Chairman of the Rescue Council of Management was Bishop Kelly, who was full of encouragement and support for enterprises benefiting the welfare of children and their families.

We learned there were only four Children's Hospices in the country at that time. These were situated in Oxford, Cambridge, Birmingham and Wetherby, the latter being the nearest Hospice for children and families of the Greater Manchester area. We visited two of these Hospices, Acorns in Birmingham and Martin House in Wetherby. In Martin House we received tremendous encouragement and support. Robin Wood, the Administrator, and Miss Lenore Hill, the Senior Nurse, filled us in with all that such an undertaking entailed and the cost of building and maintenance. Martin House was by then bursting at the seams and they thought they would need to reassess the geographical area from which they received children. The prospect of a Children's Hospice in Manchester was music to their ears!

Research into the need for Francis House went ahead; in March 1990 the decision was made by the Council to go ahead with the development of a Children's Hospice. It was agreed that the Convent of our Lady of Lourdes, which was the home of the Franciscan Missionary Sisters of St Joseph, known in the Diocese of Salford as the Rescue Sisters, be converted and extended, and the Sisters would be relocated and the building and grounds would be used by the Hospice. The Sisters vacated the Convent on 3 December 1990 and the builders moved in on the same day.

It was important that we were quickly registered by the Charity Commission as a charity independent from the Catholic Children's Rescue Society – this work had to be for children of all faiths and none, and so the Rainbow Family Trust came into being. Once registered with the Charities Commission, we were able to move forward with contacting the local Health Authority and begin fundraising, which from the very beginning was a heavy burden. During the next months we met parents, pediatricians and other professionals engaged in the care of children, and reported back at each meeting. The Hospice must provide care of the entire family and not the child in isolation. A scheme was set up in the name of Rainbow Warrior, to try to secure a future for Francis House. We failed at that time to get any backing from national press or media.

The completed building was handed over in October/November of 1991 and officially opened by HRH Princess Diana on 25 November 1991, a highlight for children, parents, staff, and for supporters of Francis House. The first children were admitted in early November.

Money continued to be a problem. In the run-up to the Millennium it was decided that a Millennium Fund should be started. It was felt that it might be feasible to raise a million pounds within the year. This was not to be. We didn't realise just how hard it was to reach such a target. The following year, 2000, Susie Mathis, who had supported Francis House from its initiation, while visiting, met Kirsty with her parents and two sisters. There was an immediate reaction between Kirsty and Susie.

All the children in Francis House are very special to us; the criteria for acceptance is that they have a life-threatening condition. Kirsty's condition, unlike the condition of many of the children, allows her to be mobile and communicate and more important, she is unafraid of cameras. Susie talked with Kirsty's parents, Steve and Lynn, and Kirsty's sisters, Zoe and Kim. Together it was agreed that the Kirsty Appeal be initiated and Kirsty be the face of and ambassador for all the children using Francis House. The Warrior and Millennium appeals were absorbed into the new one.

Through the combined efforts of Susie and Kirsty, Francis House received the national and local media cover which we simply could not attain in the early days.

I leave Kirsty and Susie to tell their own story.

WHEN I MET KIRSTY

'What's your name?'

'Kirsty'

'How old are you?'

'Four.'

Her tiny frame, delicate and doll-like, seemed impossibly fragile. She was attached by a narrow tube to an oxygen tank and I noticed her lips and fingers were blue, although at the time I had no idea why. Her eyes were huge, the most expressive I had seen. Above all, her condition – whatever it was – hadn't stopped her charging about, evoking laughter from the other children at the Francis House Children's Hospice, which is what had drawn me to her from where I had been sitting outside in the garden. Now, as we chatted, I realised Kirsty was also loving, questioning and intelligent. I began to wonder if I might just have found the answer to our problems.

The task

Not all bodies can be fixed with the tools at our disposal. Sometimes, the best the doctors can do is to manage pain and other symptoms and arrange support for the patients and their families. This is the area of medicine known as 'palliative care'.

Francis House Children's Hospice in Manchester was opened in November 1991 to provide palliative care for children with a short life expectancy. The qualifying criterion for families to receive this desperately needed care is that their child is not expected to reach adulthood. Francis House was the fifth hospice to be built and, prior to this phenomenal facility, children and their families would have to gather on hospital wards. Families were left to their own devices and counselling was not a major consideration.

Diana, Princess of Wales, opened the Hospice. It costs more than £1.5 million a year to run, at least £600,000 of which is for the highly skilled specialist care required for children and their families dealing with terminal illness. The total contribution towards these costs provided by the local authorities amounts to just £50,000 – a mere 3%. This is the best that FIVE Local Health Authorities can manage between them! And Central Government provides NOTHING. This means that just 17 days of care are covered by public funding, leaving 348 days to be covered by private fundraising.

I had been connected with Francis House from the beginning and had raised money and gained support as a presenter at Piccadilly Radio. I knew how hard it was, not just to raise £1.5 million once, but to have to raise it every year. However, I only found out just how intolerable this burden had become when one day in 1999 the administrator of Francis House, Sister Aloysius, telephoned and asked me to join her for an urgent meeting at the Hospice.

I learnt at that meeting that the annual fundraising target had become impossible to meet and that, if no other monies were forthcoming, the Hospice would last for only three more months. Sister desperately needed help to raise the profile and ultimately to secure the future of Francis House. This was not a situation that could be remedied by functions or occasional fundraising events. The Hospice would only be safe if it could secure a substantial level of base funding. How much would be required to do that? **Five million pounds**. Then, if there were a shortfall in the annual funds raised, the interest alone from the monies we had raised would act as a safety net.

It was a huge, almost overwhelming prospect and I had no idea how it could be achieved. But, when facing a selfless woman whom you admire and hold in such high regard, the word 'no' is not on your list of options.

Such was the beginning of the Rainbow Millennium Fund campaign, which has since become the Kirsty Appeal. This is the story of how we set out to raise that £5m and how the campaign was rescued and given its impetus the day I first met that one special little girl.

Where do we begin?

At the time I took that call from Sister Aloysius, my friend Phil Taylor and I were just embarking on our own business venture.

The idea was for us to earn enough money from arranging events – parties or whatever – to pay our mortgages. There was no business strategy but, as long as we enjoyed our venture, that would be good enough for us. Our office was my dining room, we used a borrowed computer and another friend donated a fax machine, while the communal desk was my kitchen table. Now, suddenly, as well as trying to make a success of the business, we were going to raise £5 million for charity!

Don't panic, I thought. It's a big number but there are lots of people out there so divide it up. Contact 2,000 people and ask them to donate £2,000 each. This would be tax-deductible and could be paid by direct debit into what was then the Rainbow Millennium Fund. Easy.

After several weeks we had managed to sign up eight people. That meant £4,984,000 to go. On to the next idea – use your contacts, bring in the professionals!

Colin Lane is the Head of Sales with the Times Newspaper Group and he offered his help. Colin was in the business of selling advertising space and told us that companies sometimes reneged on taking up space reserved for them, forcing the newspapers either to sell it at a ridiculously cheap rate or to fill the space with editorial. I was fired with enthusiasm – it seemed perfect for the Appeal.

We duly persuaded an advertising agency to help us design an ad. They came up with the muted outline of a child, as if seen through a bathroom window. The caption read: 'Just imagine, in the mind of the person looking at this ad the undefined image could be of their own child'. I wasn't completely sold but it seemed to make sense and several newspapers offered us free space when and if it became available. Finally, it appeared in *The Times*. I was overjoyed. We sat by the free phone 08000 971 197 hour on hour and it was very, very quiet; in fact the phone never bloody rang!

It was a bitter blow. We had to start again. I asked myself what motivated *me* to donate via an advert and I realised that the message had to be *tangible*. If someone was raising money for a mistreated donkey, a dancing bear or an abandoned dog, looking at them through a muted image would not have the same impact as looking at the real thing. I was convinced that what we were trying to get over had to be real, a true story, something or someone that the general public would be affected by.

Although we didn't know it, what we wanted, and what Francis House needed, was Kirsty. And that was why, when I first met her, I was so excited. However, meeting her was only part of the solution; I was now faced with another huge hurdle – and it was one we had to clear for the campaign to go ahead.

Doctors cannot help Kirsty...

How do you approach the family of a terminally ill child and tell them that you want to make her the face of an advertising campaign? I knew the cause was right and I was sure that Kirsty was the right person but how would her mother and father react? Having a terminally ill child puts an enormous strain on any family and can easily tear it apart as individuals struggle to cope. But Kirsty's background and medical problems would surely test the strongest family unit to its limit.

The Howard family – left to right: Kirsty, Steve, Kim, Lynn and Zoe.
(YFA)

Kirsty Ellen Howard was born at 9:42 a.m. on Wednesday 20 September 1995 at Wythenshawe Hospital, Manchester and weighed an apparently healthy 7lb 2oz. Shortly after her birth, her parents Steve and Lynn were told something was wrong.

As Steve remembers, 'The nurse in the recovery room monitored Kirsty's breathing, and later that day the duty doctor came to see us and told us that Kirsty may have a heart murmur. We had no idea how bad it was'.

The following day Kirsty received ultrasound to her heart and on the Friday she was rushed to the Royal Manchester Children's Hospital in Pendlebury. By that time, Lynn and Steve realised their baby's problem was more serious than had first been imagined so Lynn discharged herself from Wythenshawe to be by her daughter's side.

For the next eight months Kirsty was constantly admitted to hospital until finally she was referred to Birmingham Children's Hospital, which specialises in heart problems. There, she spent 15 days on a life-support machine suffering from bronchiolitis. Even at this stage Kirsty was a fighter and astonished the doctors by breathing by herself. But, sadly, she couldn't sustain this and needed open-heart surgery. Complications followed, leading to three more open-heart surgery procedures. Time and again she recovered, fighting her way through a total of eleven operations, including nine cardiac procedures.

Despite her strength, there was a limit to what doctors could do for a heart abnormality so rare that it has not even got a name and so severe that, simply stated, she was born with her heart 'back to front' so that all other organs are misplaced. The chances of a child being born with this condition are one in sixty million and there is only one other child in the world known to have suffered from it. The official diagnosis is as follows:

Left arterial isomerism, left verticular isomerism. Both great arteries originate from the anterior ventricle. No Superior Vena Cava on the right. Left Superior Vena Cava drains into the coronary sinus. Right pulmonary veins drain into the right-sided atrium and the left pulmonary veins drain into the left-sided atrium. The inferior vena cava is interrupted and the hepatic veins drain into the right-sided atrium

The doctors told Steve and Lynn that for the rest of her life Kirsty would have to be attached to a 45lb cylinder, supplying her oxygen 24 hours a day. She would need to be checked five times a night to ensure she was still alive. By February 1999 the medical team had determined that no further operations could be performed on Kirsty, since she would not survive the anaesthetic. Kirsty was terminally ill and could be offered only palliative care of the type offered by Francis House Children's Hospice.

It was against this background that I found myself asking Steve and Lynn and their other daughters, Zoe, born 15 June 1989 and Kim, born 12 February 1992, how they felt about Kirsty being the figurehead for our fundraising campaign.

After I outlined my plans, they agreed to ring me the next day with their decision. As Steve recalls: 'We did have a major worry and that was what would happen if Kirsty did not make it; would the appeal still go ahead? Susie's answer was emphatically "yes" – Kirsty would be the figurehead and the campaign would continue after her. We both felt that if Kirsty fronted the campaign it would mean securing Francis House and helping many other children and their families in the future. We agreed'.

Hearing this news gave us a tremendous boost. We were so keen to begin that Phil and I contacted Mark Hendley, a photographer, to get cracking right away. So it was that, for the very first time, the first of a million times, I found myself pulling Kirsty's oxygen cylinder into position for a photograph. I remember asking her to sit on the dry grass to pose. Kirsty automatically crossed her legs demurely, put her hand under her chin and delivered a smile to die for, gazing directly into the camera and piercing the lens with her phenomenal smile. What a natural!

I placed the photograph in the *Manchester Evening News's* free paper the *Metro News,* along with the freephone number 08000 971 197. With the help and fantastic support of a lovely lady called Lucy Palmer we got front page and yes, thank goodness, this time the phone started to ring.

The response to the *Metro* article gave me the confidence to go back to the advertising agency, J. Walter Thompson and convince them that *this* was the way forward; Kirsty, telling a true story, should head the campaign. They began work on the wording for the first advert and, after numerous false starts and alterations, the final *strapline* was chosen:

'Doctors cannot help Kirsty, but you can'

The Howards have my unending gratitude for letting me into their lives and putting up with me ever since. None of us knew where this journey would take us but human beings thrive on purpose and goals. Kirsty had been given only six weeks to live, but I firmly believe that being able to help our campaign has given her a sense of purpose and she has thrived ever since, by being the leading lady of her Appeal. Every new challenge, every big occasion, has been a milestone for Kirsty to strive towards and to pass. Those milestones and those successes are documented in this book and the thousands of photographs which have been taken of Kirsty since Mark Hendley captured that first image at Francis House.

I hope that what you see as you go through this book will show what the campaign has brought to Kirsty and what Kirsty has brought to the campaign.

Garden view of Francis House Children's Hospice. (MEN)

HOUSE NOT FOR SALE

Francis House, East Didsbury, Manchester

When our Campaign began, there was a very real prospect that the Hospice would close. The Kirsty Appeal exists to ensure that, whatever fluctuations may occur in the annual battle to raise revenue for the running of the Hospice, Francis House will never be reduced to the bricks and mortar of an estate agent's particulars, but will instead remain a home for children and families who need it.

No words can describe the atmosphere created within Francis House and the extremes of emotions experienced there day in, day out. Many people's perception of a children's hospice is one of overwhelming sadness and despair, but this is definitely not the reality. A hospice is a place for children to live and laugh and to love whilst they are alive, and for families to benefit from the respite and the care away from the stresses of their everyday lives.

Reception and Day Lounge

The first thing you notice is the warmth and welcome from lovely Carmel at the reception. This area is usually littered with cuddly toys and it is home to the Hospice goldfish. You then enter a huge communal day lounge. The sounds are varied – children's laughter, the TV showing the latest cartoon or video, the carers carrying out their duties chatting away to children or parents. Uniforms can create a barrier so the care team, headed by Margaret Hickey and Sister Maureen, dress normally apart from their badges. The day-lounge is the heart of the Hospice and children in all stages of their illnesses are welcomed into this room, whether in a bed, wheelchair, hammock, padded comfy seats or on bean bags; anything goes as long as the children are happy.

As soon as you are prepared to face the reality of terminal illness you realise that, although it has to encompass within itself the most tragic of situations, Francis House remains a haven that is uplifting, inspiring, thought-provoking, educational and yes – fun!

Snoozalam

This room is my personal favourite; a special place where children come to explore their senses, realising that, if they touch the soft objects that lie there with any part of their body, they will hear music and see changing patterns of coloured light; a safe, light-sensory environment, achieved through strands of fibre optics on a soft, padded floor.

If a room like this could tell the story of the people who had come within its walls, what a story that would be! This inspirational room gives comfort, not just to the children, but to other family members, carers and all who come to Francis House.

It is a place where, when you need quiet, you can just close your eyes and drift.

Music Room

The Music Room at Francis House is actually quite small, but the work that goes on within its walls is immense. The music teacher, a wonderful lady called Brigitte, works individually with each child and also, from time to time, organises and orchestrates the most amazing musical interludes. Each adult and child is given a musical instrument of a wind or percussion variety, while Brigitte herself conducts and co-ordinates – magical!

The room also contains, despite the limited space, a grand piano. It is worth pausing for a moment to tell you a little about its history and about a girl called Sarah.

The Times newspaper in London generously offered five thousand pounds to buy something we needed for the Hospice. But what should it be? Objects we don't need, toys we don't need; rocking horses breed in our Hospice! Naturally people want to buy whatever is needed to make the children happy and it is equally natural to assume that *things* are what we need for that purpose. What people may not realise is that it is the care team who do most to make the children happy and it is the cost of maintaining that team which accounts for the bulk of what we have to raise each year. On this occasion, however, Sister Aloysius decided that she wanted a grand piano.

I confess I was shocked. My image of a grand piano was that of an elitist object suited for a great aristocratic residence or a grand concert hall. How wrong I was! I will never in my life forget the moment when I witnessed the grand piano at its instrumental best.

I had met Sarah previously and one would imagine, given the number of visits that I have made to the Hospice, I would become immune to the different severities of illness. But this one day shocked me to the core. As I moved through our family room, where on any one day there are beds, hammocks, chairs, and music therapy, communal fun and communal empathy, I was stopped in my tracks by Sarah.

In front of me there was a cosy bed, enveloping a little girl with upsetting disfigurement. Unbelievably and unjustly, a girl at the tender age of five was actually going through puberty. Her eyes gazed towards a rotating aerial mobile placed where she could see it. Feeling strongly that I wanted to communicate with her and take her gaze away from the ceiling, I spoke, and her entire face became redder and redder and she started to shake uncontrollably. I asked Sister Maureen what I was doing wrong. I was told that the little girl was just so happy that I was there. Sarah seldom communicated.

Opening the door of the Music Room the day after we had received the grand piano, I was privileged to see Sarah experiencing a unique, quiet moment of complete contentment. As she lay on a white furry blanket, she could feel the vibration of the music coming through from the piano. I thought I had seen everything but this was amazing: Sarah, with all her problems, was benefiting enormously from Sister Aloysius's grand piano.

Teenagers' Lounge

When the new extension to Francis House was built, it was felt that there was a desperate need for a Teenagers' Lounge. Because the prognosis for many terminally ill children is entirely unpredictable, many children thankfully become young adults and they choose to continue respite at Francis House.

This is quite simply a room for teenagers to do whatever teenagers do. It is equipped with TV, sound system and all the hi-tech gadgets of the sort that any normal teenager would surround themselves with.

While many of the teenagers are wheelchair-bound, it is important that they should enjoy as much independence as possible, to be allowed to grow as individuals and to experience the adolescent lifestyle. The carers in this area are exceptional; they have a great understanding of each child's individual needs, which ensures that their respite is a happy experience.

Chapel

The chapel, which of course is non-denominational, is dominated by a huge stained-glass rainbow, where the sun filters through, casting a prism of light over the quiet interior. On entering by the heavy door, I am always struck at once by the aura. One is immediately aware of a thousand prayers that have been offered here and the emotions of the people who have passed through that very door, which after all these years I still cannot master.

People always comment on the beautiful child-like tapestry hanging behind the altar and there, to its right are three Books of Memories. Look through them and as the pages unfold, you will come to appreciate just how many children, of all backgrounds, denominations and cultures have been cared for as they came to the end of their little lives here at Francis House.

Yet, in the face of tragedy, so many of the most uplifting experiences have taken place in this chapel. Father Tom has delivered full sermons without mentioning the word God – Love at the time has been far more understood by some of the parents of a little one who has passed away.

There are so many wonderful services throughout the year but a favourite by far is the Midnight Service on Christmas Eve. On this festive occasion, Sister Austin and Sister Aloysius join families, while children, however poorly, join together with the dedicated congregation, all of whom are praying for hope and strength. Afterwards, we welcome Christmas Day with sherry and mince pies.

The Rainbow Rooms

The Rainbow Rooms are actually mortuaries. These are the rooms that will be the final resting place within Francis House for children with terminal illnesses. It is here where families whom the carers have known, laughed with, had fun with and cried with, have to try to come to terms with their loss.

I hope I have shown you that Francis House is not a place of overwhelming sadness but, as in the world at large, we are all faced ultimately with the fact of mortality and tears will be shed. Tears will never be more poignant than those that fall in the Rainbow Rooms.

The Hospice book of memories. (MEN)

IN THE LIMELIGHT

It was not long before I realised that the limelight suited Kirsty. Via Cavendish Press, the *Sunday People* picked up on her story and decided to run with it. The initial pieces were over-sensationalised and upsetting for the Howard family, but they did grab the public's attention. The paper's chief writer, Rachael Bletchly, along with the editor, Neil Wallis, started their own appeal on our behalf with phenomenal success. The story led directly to a call I received at home from a lady called Belinda White.

At that time Belinda was in charge of the Al Fayed Charitable Trust and was ringing on behalf of Mr Mohamed Al Fayed himself. I could hardly contain my excitement when she explained her purpose. He was thinking of donating a large sum of money to the Hospice! Belinda visited the Hospice within weeks and the subsequent fantastic £120,000 cheque arrived along with an invitation for Kirsty to visit Harrods. This was the largest single donation the Hospice had ever received and a significant advancement for our campaign. It was also the start of a very special relationship between Kirsty and Mr Al Fayed.

Kirsty was already proving tremendously popular with the media, but I realised we could not sit back and wait for journalists to come to us. If the future of Francis House was to be secured, we needed the ongoing support of the media – and we had to give the journalists what they wanted. My first target was the Editor of the *Manchester Evening News* (MEN).

This is no ordinary local paper. Celebrities and businesses alike know that if they appear in the MEN, they will gain respect and recognition for their good work. I tried and failed many times to entice Paul Horrocks to become involved, and finally succeeded at a networking party. I had to leave the occasion early to attend a charity event but, on my way out, I brushed past Mr Horrocks and took the opportunity to ask him to visit the Hospice. To my delight he responded with those

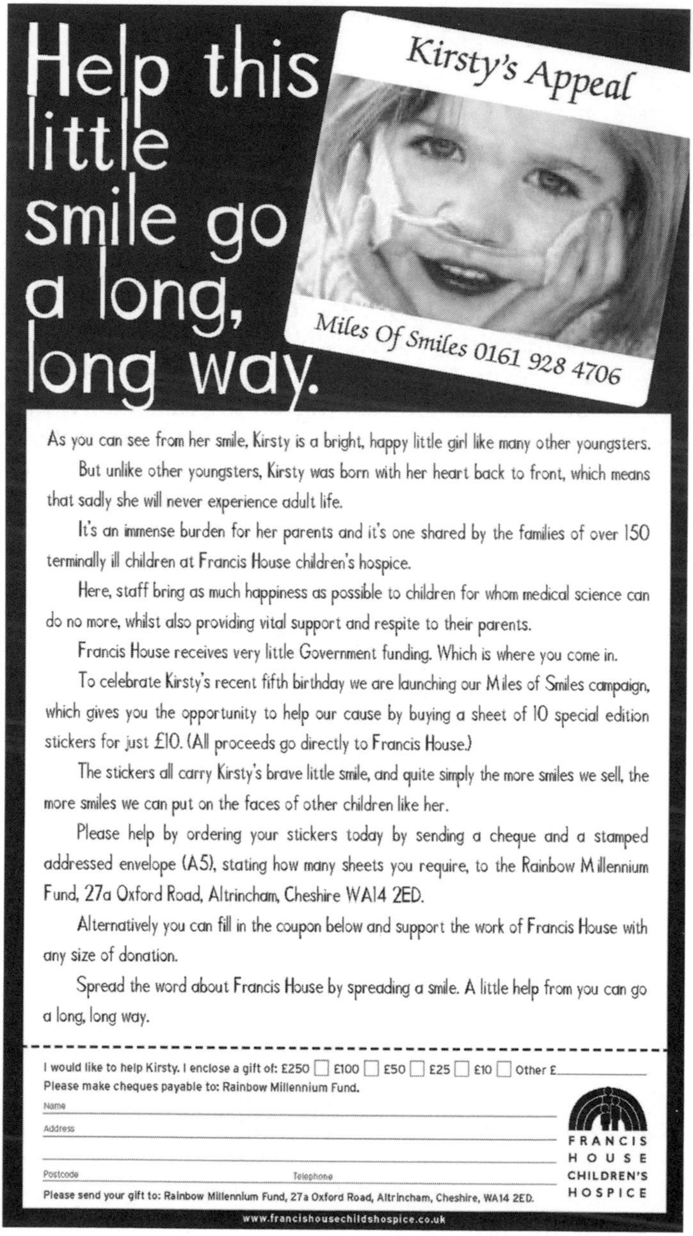

Kirsty advertises the Appeal. (CB JWT)

wonderful positive words, 'Phone my secretary and make the meeting'. Even though there wasn't a gap in the diary for six weeks, somehow an appointment was made.

Once you have taken someone through its doors, Francis House does not require a hard sell, especially when Kirsty reaches out two tiny arms to be picked up. She herself actually organised the tour of the ground floor and, as Paul and I left her in the lounge and entered the quiet stairwell, it was clear that he was visibly moved by our special haven. He asked me there and then what I wanted from him and this led to Paul becoming a Patron and the *Manchester Evening News* making Kirsty's Appeal its own. Since then Paul's unstinting support has been the bedrock of our Campaign, helping us to reach not only local businesses and celebrities but also, and most important, the people of the North West.

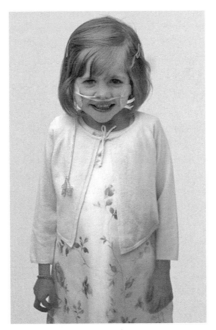

Kirsty poses for the lottery
advertisement for Cheetham Bell JWT.
(PM CB JWT)

Meanwhile, pictures of Kirsty gave focus to a whole string of advertisements in the national media, as we campaigned for further donations. New straplines were tried, some better than others, but Kirsty was the common thread and hers was fast becoming the face of children's hospices. But advertisements mean little unless the public is aware of the story behind the picture. That meant getting press coverage.

An obvious approach was to set about arranging events involving Kirsty, which would attract media interest. But no matter how noble the cause, newspapers will only print stories if you give them a good angle. These cannot be arranged overnight and Kirsty's precarious health meant we never knew if she would be well enough to take part in whatever had been planned.

At this point you may well ask why we were concentrating so much on donations from the public at large. What about Government and the various charitable foundations? We lobbied MPs to support improved funding for children's hospices, both through local authorities, and by extra funding from central government, for palliative care within a children's hospice. For whatever reason, our efforts have failed, despite the fact that, as we shall see, Kirsty took the fight all the way up to Tony Blair!

We were no more successful with our numerous letters to charitable trusts. Sister Aloysius and the Hospice Treasury Committee have applied and been refused lottery funds on three separate occasions. The actual applications involve so much time and effort and it is heartbreaking, when you realise that the whole process has been for nothing. This was so much so that, at the next meeting with our advertising partners (by this time known as Cheetham Bell J Walter Thompson), we decided to go for a thought-provoking dig at lottery funding. If the Lottery had no money for dying children then we could use its very failure to support us as a fundraising tool and shame them into the bargain.

Russ Vine and his creative team injected a new enthusiasm towards achieving our goals. The advertisement pictured our girl holding a ticket for the National Lottery and the strapline to go with it was hard-hitting and controversial.

The very first picture of Kirsty as the leading lady of her Appeal. (MH)

'The only way a terminally ill child like Kirsty will benefit from the lottery is if she wins it'

The major response came from the *Sunday People*, exposing the Lottery for allocating monies to causes which in some cases appeared downright unworthy. The only response from the Lottery Commission was a phone call from a gentleman at the Press Office, asking me to withdraw the ad, as it discredited their chosen beneficiaries! By the end of the call he was giving me the name of the Lottery's personal charitable trust, so that I could write to them for support. I did write, and guess what? No reply!

Harrods – London, here we come!!

The personal invitation from Mr Al Fayed to visit Harrods was extremely exciting for Kirsty and the Howard family. This was the first trip to the capital for everyone in the family, apart from Steve, whose regiment had been sent there in the '70s, to provide a substitute firefighting force during the industrial troubles.

Two concentrators, seven oxygen cylinders, metres of leads – organisation of this first trip was going to be a major logistical exercise. Firstly, although Mr Al Fayed had offered to pay for the transportation, we needed to find someone empathetic and reliable enough to meet the Howard family's needs. I phoned several private hire companies and, after a few 'who cares who it is', I was lucky enough to happen upon a lovely family in Cheshire. They had a disabled little boy named Matthew and therefore understood the difficulties and problems that disability can bring. I could tell from our conversation that theirs would be a genuine offer of help. Their quote was so reasonable and that day a very special relationship was formed with our new driver. Kirsty nicknamed him Roger the Dodger!

Kirsty and Victoria Beckham open the Harrods sale on 4 January 2002.
(HPO)

Mr Al Fayed had generously invited us all to stay as his guests at an address known to us only as the dark blue square on a Monopoly Board – Park Lane! The entrance to number 55 (sandwiched between the Grosvenor House Hotel and the Ferrari showroom) was decked with elegant white Christmas trees, whilst stylish uniformed concierges were on hand to greet Kirsty. Wow! She had arrived!

The Howards were given a stunning three-bedroomed apartment, all *en suite*, overlooking Hyde Park, decorated with Elizabethan furnishings; huge chandeliers glistened above the elaborate rooms. The square footage of this apartment must have put it among the most prime real estate in London. In the kitchen there was the most amazing floor-to-ceiling fridge, stocked with Harrods produce – pastrami, yogurts, mineral water, speciality jams, smoked salmon. Phil and I were staggered by Mr Al Fayed's generosity but Lynn took one look and exclaimed 'What no Carling?!' You can take the girl out of Northern Moor but you can't take the Northern Moor out of the girl, as Lynn would happily acknowledge.

The next morning, we dressed and I washed Kirsty's hair; by now I was becoming quite good at blow-drying. We left with Roger to meet Father Christmas, or do I mean Mr Al Fayed? – For us they were one and the same! Arriving at door number 10 of Harrods we were escorted to the opulent Georgian restaurant, where socialites 'do lunch'. On the majestic grand piano the gentleman was playing *They can't take that away from me*, and no one could take that moment away from us.

Mr Al Fayed arrived on the fifth floor, flanked by four huge security men, but in a flash every guard was dropped as Kirsty approached him. It's strange, but Kirsty always seems to do exactly what is needed in any situation. Within seconds she was in the great man's arms. The security men showered her with dolls and presents, she giggled and he glowed. She was totally oblivious to the fact that he was the owner of the most famous store in the world; she just saw a man with a kind face who was taking her to see Father Christmas.

Kirsty, Zoe and Kim were all photographed with this fantastic Santa and with Mr Al Fayed. As we left the grotto, something very special took place. Tiny Kirsty began pulling at the back of Mr Al Fayed's jacket, he turned and found Kirsty raising her arms high, inviting him to pick her up and hold her. As he did so, the tears rolled down his face and in that moment a real and special bond was formed between them.

The following February, Mr Al Fayed made a special trip by private 'plane to Francis House. Sadly one of the children had passed away that morning. Though the privacy of Natalie's family was paramount at this tragic time, we knew that our special guests would now witness first-hand, not just the fantastic haven that was Francis House, but also the harsh realities and profound sadness that families have to endure.

Mr Al Fayed arrived laden with gifts: there were cuddly bears, DVDs, widescreen TV, golden chocolate bars – the children were amazed. Once settled, Kirsty grabbed his hand and proceeded to show him Francis House Children's Hospice. He was extremely moved and, after the tour, spent a quiet time with Natalie's bereaved parents.

After the photo-shoot that day, the picture that made all the papers was an unsolicited cheeky action from Kirsty as she took a £20 note from the top pocket of his jacket. By this time, he had pledged a lot more than that £20; he had committed to donating £5,000 a month from his Harrods Charitable Trust in perpetuity.

Mohamed Al Fayed's emotions on his visit to the Hospice and especially his feelings for Kirsty are abundantly clear when you look at the photograph.

Kirsty meets the Prime Minister

The Kirsty Appeal needs the Press and so do politicians. Neil Wallis, the editor of the *Sunday People,* told us at the close of 2000 that Alistair Campbell had spoken positively about a trip to Downing Street for Kirsty and a portfolio of our campaign was prepared for him. Kirsty meeting Tony Blair was news.

'You must be Kirsty,' he said, greeting us behind the most famous front door in the world. Quite unabashed, Kirsty walked right up to the Prime Minister, took hold of his hand and replied 'You must be Tony'. Then, as the two of them walked hand in hand into the White Room to meet the rest of our party for Jammie Dodgers and afternoon tea, Kirsty told

Kirsty knocks at No 10 – lucky policeman! (MS P)

him, 'You have a very posh house!' I'll never forget her settling into the huge chair once occupied by Sir Winston Churchill.

I am sure we all had our own agendas that day. Mine was clear and focused. I doubted I was ever going to have another opportunity to speak to the Prime Minister, and to make the case for better funding for children's hospices.

'Where is the help from the Government?' I pleaded. At this point he turned to his PA. 'Please get me all the information on children's hospices, to be on my desk on Monday morning'. I really thought we'd done it. He was listening! I virtually skipped out of that house – I could not wait to get back to the hotel to celebrate.

The pictures speak for themselves but, nearly six years later, we are still waiting for any difference. I have continued to write to Mr Blair, not only to plead with him to make extra provision for children's hospices, but also to invite him to each milestone celebration. We always receive polite acknowledgements of our letters from his secretary, but nothing ever comes of it. I would hate to think that Tony Blair felt nothing at all on the day I sat with him and told him the truth about children's hospices. I would hate to think that he was just staging a scene from *Yes, Prime Minister* when he called for the papers on his desk on Monday morning. But Government should be judged by results and we have had no results.

I said that we all had an agenda that day and that mine was clear. Only Tony Blair can say for sure what his agenda was.

The Million Pound Party

Fundraising, however important, can sometimes be a thankless task, so it is really important to celebrate the landmarks. A constant source of motivation is watching Phil add to a huge whiteboard the latest monies banked for the Kirsty Appeal. I never really appreciated how many thousands it took to reach a million but watching the total slowly grow in 0's made that first million an occasion for a momentous celebration.

Coincidentally the chosen date, 31 July 2001, was also the 28th birthday of one of our then patrons, Tracy Shaw, and she graciously forfeited her own party to share it with Kirsty. Tracy was an A list celebrity which guaranteed great press coverage. The observatory of the Radisson Hotel was our chosen location. My friend Adam Evanson worked a miracle and the hotel supplied the food free of charge, with an excellent discount for the champagne and other liquid refreshments. This was the beginning of a great PR event and a huge party. We managed to get a complimentary room for the Howards and, with the £1 million cake and balloons, we were on our way. One thing you learn when continually begging is the importantance of always saying thank you; if nothing else it allows you to ask again.

Sister Aloysius, Sister Austin, Father Tom, our patrons and their partners, Russ Vine and the team from Cheetham Bell, Rachael and Martin from the *Sunday People*, all sang happy birthday to Tracy. One arrival who made a huge impact on the event was the much-loved, late and sadly missed Frank Lammar, who was himself going through a traumatic time with his own illness. He was so touched by Kirsty, his eyes filled with tears as she was photographed with Tracy blowing out the candles on her cake. I don't think that there are many little girls who have played such a big part in raising one million pounds but Frank definitely knew how that felt.

Patron Tracy Shaw shares her birthday, to celebrate Kirsty's first £1 million. (MEN)

After the usual speeches, acknowledgements and thanks, Kirsty started the first of many renditions of her favourite Ronan Keating song, *I Love You Best When You Say Nothing at All*. The sight I love best, even above front-page colour photographs and the emotions they engender, is a prominent display of the Appeal's freephone contact number, because publicity, however massive, does not guarantee an increase in our donations unless people know where they can donate.

So only £4 million to go. . . .

THE BECKHAM CONNECTION

England v Greece – Manchester United 6 October 2001
Kirsty, however fragile and ill, has the interests and passions of any normal healthy child.

She is a Manchester United fan; she is red through and through and, when I realised that goals, in every sense of the word, were an inspiration for her, I tried to find a way for her to be a mascot for a Manchester United match. This never happened, but instead, our efforts resulted in an uplifting phone call several weeks later from Paul Barber, the Marketing Director of the Football Association. 'Will the England – Greece game be OK?' he asked, 'and will Kirsty walk out hand in hand with David Beckham?'.

Oh boy, that was a phone call I will never forget. How was I ever to keep this a secret? I decided not to tell anyone but Phil, until we had received the final confirmation, so I held that secret until Kirsty's 6th birthday on 20 September 2001, two weeks before the match. Her expression was extraordinary; a mixture of excitement and shock. She looked at me and said, 'With Beckham, with David, with David, with Beckham?'.

The date of the match, 6 October, was getting towards winter; it was cold, what if it rained? What if she was not well enough to do it? It simply might not happen, due to Kirsty's fragility. Two criteria guide us always; not only must the event represent something that really makes Kirsty happy and excited, but also she must feel well enough to follow it through.

When the big day came it was indeed quite cold but at least there was no sign of rain as I arrived at Old Trafford, to meet Kirsty and family at the Sir Matt Busby entrance. We met a lovely lady called Sue at the reception and she looked after the extra oxygen cylinders. We made our way round to the designated area for changing. The mascot wears the strip of the opposing team and I was handed the kit for Kirsty, which unfortunately was a size intended for nine-year-olds. At the

Kirsty and the England squad on 6 October 2001. (AIL)

time Kirsty fitted into clothes designed for a 3–4 year old, so it was a good job that I had brought plenty of layers of tights and thermal underwear, to assure insulation for Kirsty and to pad out the Greek strip. We Sang *Hey Baby* and danced to try to keep warm whilst the volume outside increased.

And then we felt the tunnel come alive. They were coming.

David Beckham walked through on his way to the pitch for the warm-up and, as he reached the alcove, he stopped and simply said 'Hello Kirsty'. She forgot about the temperature. 'Hello David' she said, stretching out her arms for him to hold her. He did what we all hope our heroes will do and held her in his strong arms. He said he was going to have a kick-about and he would be back. Kirsty came back into my arms and we resumed singing *Hey Baby* with extra vigour.

I could scarcely believe it; Kirsty did not even turn her head or look back for any reassurance. She just walked on, hand in hand with her hero. Beckham and his team did not stride out that day as strong athletes. Instead, they entered the arena together, at the pace of our tiny, terminally ill little girl, Kirsty. That sight will be remembered by many thousands of people and it is one that I certainly will remember forever. How many children have you seen walk out as a mascot and not learnt one thing about them? I spent a lot of time to make sure the viewers knew exactly who Kirsty was, and fortunately, that persistence paid off, because John Motson in his match commentary delivered his words with such emotion; he said 'Here's the real hero of the team and it's not a footballer it is an extraordinary little girl and her name is Kirsty'.

The world's press wanted a team photograph and so David and the boys all knelt down ready to pose, never knowing how important this particular photograph would be to Kirsty. To this day it is her favourite and, when you ask her why it is so special, she answers simply 'Because they are all at the same height as me'.

Kirsty watched the rest of the match with the crowd and, when Beckham bent the ball into the net to send England to the World Cup, he dedicated the goal to his greatest fan.

Kirsty was certainly David's good luck charm that day, so much so that he called her from Japan the night before the game with Brazil.

England mascot Kirsty with her hero, David Beckham, at the England v Greece qualifier for the World Cup, 6 October 2001. AIL)

'Hello Kirsty, it's only David. I'm just giving you a quick call to say Thank You so much for the pictures you have done for me.

'I've seen some pictures in the paper of you and you look absolutely gorgeous as usual. It's the night before the Brazil match, so I am just about to go to bed, it's about quarter past ten which is early for me, so I'm going to get an early night and hopefully we are going to win tomorrow for you.

'Thank you again from me and all the players and we are all wishing you well and wish you were here with us, but hopefully we will see you soon.

Love you loads'.

David and Victoria Beckham join Kirsty at her 2001 Angel Ball at the Radisson SAS, Manchester Airport. (MEN)

The Beckhams and the Angel Ball 2001

To be associated with David Beckham is an enormous publicity coup for any charitable campaign and it was imperative at that moment that we should make the most of our good fortune. Later, I asked David if he would be able to attend Kirsty's Angel Ball in November 2001, our largest and highest profile event of the year. To my surprise and delight he happily agreed to come along with Victoria.

Although I was held to secrecy, the Press were there as a matter of course and in seconds there was a furore, as they all clambered to find the best position for the right shot. We live in the north of England and are always at a disadvantage against southern hospices and charities; it was fantastic that a Manchester hospice could get the national coverage that Kirsty deserved and which we needed to support our appeal.

The Ball raised £60,000. If we had been able to announce that the Beckhams would be attending, yes, the tickets would have been worth a fortune but of course, the couple were such hot property that their attendance could not be advertised. Never mind. Such frustrations were not for Kirsty. This was her Ball and she was spending it on the lap of her hero.

Commonwealth Games – June 2002

The announcement that Manchester was to be hosting the Commonwealth Games was greeted with a degree of cynicism in some quarters, and it was not long before the pessimists from around the country were questioning whether the City could pull it off. By this time, as an adoptive Mancunian, I had become so proud of Manchester that we wanted to see the City triumph with the Games, and it seemed to us both obvious and appropriate that our little, local hero should be at the centre of that triumph.

When you are promoting a charity, however, nothing is achieved without hard work and passionate commitment. Phil and I were still all that comprised the fundraising office for the Kirsty Appeal and my role centred on promoting our star. This meant not only reacting to opportunities but actively seeking them out. How wonderful would it be for Kirsty if we could find a place for her in such a key event for the history of her native City!

As soon as it was announced where the Games were to be held, I immediately started making phone calls. This was some eighteen months before the Opening Ceremony in which Kirsty was destined to play such a prominent part. At first I was told that children must be over ten to be involved, so I asked

*David Beckham and Kirsty at the opening ceremony for the
Commonwealth Games, in Manchester, 25 July 2002. (MEN)*

whether Kirsty could give a posy to the Queen; there had to be
some part that she could play.

Despite her own unique qualities and all the wonderful help
we had received to make her a national figure, it looked as if we
were getting nowhere, until suddenly a call came from Sue
Woodward of Granada, who had been chosen to organise the
programming. I was about to undergo surgery and could not
attend the meeting but my last words to Phil from the hospital
bed were 'Don't come away until she has a starring role!'.

The meeting went well but the familiar message came across
that the organisers hoped that David or Victoria might play a

part. This was bad timing for us, since David was playing in the World Cup and we had no way of speaking directly to him, while his office sounded discouraging to say the least. So we waited and held our breath. I was so scared that, if we did not manage to get David on board, Kirsty's own involvement would be in jeopardy but, as the weeks went by, the organisers kept in touch, always in a positive way, and then they asked us to go in for a final meeting.

Phil and I still had no idea whether we could deliver the England Captain, so we asked if the organisers would recognise that Kirsty was, in any event, the right person to represent Manchester at this unique and special occasion. As we drove up towards the new stadium out hearts were in our mouths, little knowing that we were about to experience probably the most emotional moment of our campaign.

The Director, David Zolkwer, Sue Woodward and Di Hendry all sat round a table drinking mineral water. We talked about the event and explained that we had not heard from David, that Victoria was now heavily pregnant and would not be available to attend. After speaking about the wonderful merits of Kirsty, I faced the Director, looked into his eyes and waited for what he had to say. His words when they came were the most magical that I have ever heard. He said that, when the moment came for the baton to be passed to the Queen – after 6,000 people from all around the world had played their part – at that key moment the person needed to represent Manchester was someone who had demonstrated the strength and courage to overcome all adversities to meet their goals, the very qualities needed for the highest achievements in sport and in life. That person was Kirsty, with or without David Beckham!

I cried. I ran round the table and hugged everyone (though I hope these wonderful people will forgive me for declaring that I would have hugged Quasimodo if in the room at that moment). This was such a proud moment; the greatest sporting event in our City was to be spearheaded by our little girl. David and Sue then took us up to see the stadium and the site was awesome; I had goosebumps on goosebumps. We were given the dates for the rehearsals and were told that they would be writing to the Queen, asking her to break protocol by walking down the steps to meet Kirsty because Kirsty could not walk up the steps to meet her. When we left that day, we were on such a high. In only six weeks Kirsty would be meeting the Queen and opening the Commonwealth Games!

Even as the date drew nearer, I was reluctant to tell Kirsty and her family just what a major role she was scheduled to play. There had been fresh worries about her health, although these were now subsiding and her spirits were high. Only Sister Aloysius had been told; she was very excited but sworn to secrecy.

Playing the part of Kirsty at rehearsals, I kept looking around the stadium, worried that it might not be finished in time. The atmosphere was buzzy, exciting, electrifying as we ran through the final build-up, in which seven famous sports personalities, one by one, would run a part of the circumference of the stadium, each passing the baton to the next, until the last of them handed it to Kirsty for whom was reserved the honour of presenting it to Her Majesty the Queen.

From the stands Phil and I sat watching the full build-up – hundreds of children, bands, pop groups, fireworks, hot air balloons and all manner of wondrous things, building up to the final presentation. Our call took me to the place where Kirsty would receive the baton and I ceremoniously handed it to the 'Queen' so that she could read from the scroll contained within it. Even the rehearsal was spine-tingling excitement but then, as I walked away, Sue Woodward came up and whispered 'David's doing it but don't tell a soul'. I am great at keeping secrets but I wanted to shout it from the rooftops, I was so excited. It was magnificent news and going home that night Phil and I were like excited parents looking forward to Kirsty receiving the baton from her hero.

The day arrived and Manchester was awash with excitement. Anyone who was anyone was at that ceremony and everyone else was watching it on TV. The security was enormous but, once Roger the Dodger had parked and been scanned for bombs, we were taken in a golf buggy to the stadium. All the people we passed, whether they were with a school, in a band or in a choir, were shouting 'Kirsty, Kirsty!' and Kirsty waved at everyone; she was in such great spirits.

The organisers had made a special little tracksuit for her and she looked beautiful, with her little white trousers and her Cadbury's logo, her hair shining, long and straight and her face just glowing with excitement. She is a little bit like Tinkerbell; the more people clap, the more she shines. Our buggy transported us from a lounge packed with celebrities to the nearest entrance, where there were hundreds of women from the choir that would to sing with Russell Watson. Again Kirsty's fame was evident, as everyone wanted to see her, speak to her and touch her as we made our way through, then took our seats to wait for the call to enter the stadium. No more rehearsals; this was the real thing.

I turned to Kirsty who was snuggled against my body, 'Are you worried about the weight of the baton?' I asked.

'A bit.'

We had tried her with something that weighed the same and it had been fine, provided that she did not have to hold it for long. Of course, this was no longer a problem so I told her

'Kirsty, don't worry; someone you love will be handing you that baton.'

Her eyes widened and she screamed.

'David, is it David, is it David?' and I told her that it was.

Our call came to move into the stadium, waiting to be taken to the actual spot where Kirsty was to meet David. Russell Watson and the enormous choir had finished singing and the last echoes were reverberating around the arena. Then a quite incredible scene unfolded in front of us, like something from *Close Encounters*. The most enormous balloon, delicately holding a fragile acrobat, moved with the wind across the skyline. It was as if everybody in the stadium held their breath as the acrobat floated down to the centre of the arena. She descended with all the elegance and grace of Isadora Duncan and then passed the baton to Denise Lewis.

Music sounded as the seven heroes of sport brought the ceremony to its climax. Each athlete ran their part of the track and the crowd cheered as the baton was handed from hero to hero. As the fifth athlete was called to the centre of the track, we made our way to our position. How Kirsty could stand the excitement I do not know; my own heart was scarcely beating as

David Beckham helps Kirsty hand the baton to HM the Queen,

I placed the tiny girl in the centre of the track and whispered to her,

'David will be here in just a few moments and I will be right behind you.'

It was like *Chariots of Fire* as the large screens showed David taking the baton and running that final course. The applause was deafening. From the far distance he moved swiftly towards us like some classical vision of Apollo; everything about him shone – his face, his hair, his eyes, his smile as he ran towards Kirsty. As he came yet nearer her arms slowly lifted towards him and the look on his face is something I will treasure until the day that I die. There are cynics out there who like to think that people like David calculate everything in terms of public image or personal gain

But there was nothing calculated about that look and no thought of the cameras as the fragile little girl and her sporting hero were reunited in a show of mutual love and admiration. That may be why it was a moment which seemed to affect every watcher throughout the world; that union touched one billion people.

And then the realities; as David took her hand to lead her towards the podium where the Queen would meet them, I realised that Kirsty's tube was on the wrong side but unabashed, she simply flicked it over her head with her usual aplomb, and off the two of them went to meet the Queen.

What came next will always seem strange to me, not because of anything that happened but because of what did not happen. The Sovereign meets so many people of so many types from around the world and has a reputation for being able to relate to all of them. It was therefore a complete amazement to me that Her Majesty said nothing to either Kirsty or David; not even a simple platitude – aren't you brave, aren't you pretty? There was a smile from the Queen that was clearly genuine and it remains an immensely proud moment, but a puzzling one. That she didn't find something to say at that moment, I'll never understand. During the rigmarole that followed, a chosen representative opened the baton and removed the scroll for the Queen to read.

Kirsty and I left the podium and made our way back behind the stage. David was lovely and gave me a dutiful kiss and asked how I was and then spent a private moment with Kirsty before his entourage hurried him off.

From that high point, we went back to the VIP enclosure and all the celebrities that had been involved throughout the evening greeted Kirsty as if they felt privileged to be playing their part in her happiness the whole evening. As I went home that night I myself could not have been happier or prouder or more excited. I was in raptures and so proud of Manchester and what they had achieved in the organising of that magnificent ceremony, but above all I was proud of a tiny little girl who once again had touched the world with her courage.

The next morning I cannot remember waking up or getting out of bed. I think I just threw a coat on and ran out to get the papers. Back home, as I lay them out in front of me, it was surreal to see our little girl on the front pages. The pictures in *The Times*, particularly, depicted exactly what had happened and bore witness to the remarkable empathy between David and Kirsty. Whenever that opening ceremony is remembered, Kirsty will be the person who will stand out in most people's memories.

The first call that day was from Sue Woodward, who had campaigned to support us and spoke so highly of our little girl at the press conferences; I thanked the Lord that Kirsty had played her part so well for Sue and for all the organisers who had put their faith in her. After that the telephones never stopped. We only have two lines in the office and our personal mobiles, but still I have never heard so many ringing tones in one day; so many congratulations for Kirsty, so many offers of support and many, many newspapers wanting follow-up news stories about our little star.

Those next few days were crazy and we never stopped but once again profile, no matter how high, is very difficult to turn into hard cash. You can be front page in all the newspapers and people will assume this means a massive boost to your Appeal but, unless they print your full charity details and a contact number, it is little more than a lost photo opportunity for the fundraiser; so how do you evaluate the real importance of these wonderful high profile moments? This has been one the most difficult aspects of the Campaign.

Our biggest problem, perhaps, has been making sure that the high profile of the Kirsty Appeal does not actually detract from the work of the other fundraisers, earnestly seeking support for the day-to-day running of Francis House. The Kirsty Appeal exists entirely to establish the £5 million pound fund needed to ensure the long-term future of our special haven, and our cherished aim in promoting Kirsty has been to reach that target in her lifetime, as a lasting memorial to her courage, and as a legacy for the cause which has given such purpose and meaning to a life attenuated by terminal illness.

It was always our hope that the increased knowledge and appreciation of Francis House and the children's hospice movement, arising out of our own high–profile campaign, would also give increased impetus to that day-to-day fundraising, which continues separately as it did before we ever began. At the same time it is important that people do not gain the impression that the day-to-day revenue raisers do not need contributions, because capital is building up in the Kirsty Appeal Fund. If we allowed that Fund to be used up in daily running costs, we would inevitably fail to meet the purpose for which it was begun and, sooner or later, another financial crisis would arise similar to that which saw the Hospice threatened with closure in three months. We cannot and will not allow that to happen.

WINNING WAYS

Woman's Own Child of Courage – 3 December 2001

The Woman's Own Children of Courage Awards are given annually to all kinds of children who have shown great bravery. Many have performed acts of extraordinary heroism, others have endured pain and suffering as a result of disability or illness, while some have selflessly devoted their young lives to caring for members of their family.

After two years of nominating Kirsty, we were delighted when she was chosen, to be recognised at the 28th Children of Courage Awards ceremony at Westminster Abbey. Here was another big occasion, another goal for Kirsty to look forward to. It got even better – Victoria, who had been entranced by Kirsty at the Ball, was kind enough to agree to come and support her.

On the day before the award ceremony, the children were given the opportunity to meet a real prince at Buckingham Palace! The heir to the throne met the award winners and gave Kirsty a copy of a book he had written. Now, Kirsty is not fazed by anyone, including Prince Charles. He had been kneeling down for about five minutes talking to her and had started to read the book aloud, when she turned round to the future King of England and said simply 'I have had enough of you. Goodbye'. He laughed and walked off leaving Steve, Kirsty's Dad, wishing that 'the ground would swallow him up'.

The following day everyone watched Kirsty walk up with Victoria to collect her Child of Courage accolade at the Abbey ceremony. After the reception we made our way to a fabulous party in the House of Commons on the Thames embankment. Victoria, her parents and Brooklyn joined Steve, Lynn, Zoe and Kim. There were celebrities from all the TV shows that we love, pop singers, presenters, sport stars and Father Christmas. Phil and I tucked ourselves away on a small table next to Gary Rhodes. The party ended, but the excitement did not. The next morning's Press was phenomenal and tremendously helpful to the Appeal.

4 January 2002 – Harrods' Sale

At the beginning of 2002 Kirsty had another date to keep with Victoria Beckham. Our great patron, Mr Al Fayed, had invited Kirsty and Victoria to open the Harrods' Sale.

Early in the morning, when we arrived at Harrods Door 10, there were already hundreds of people around the store. We felt sorry for the opera singer, Lesley Garrett who, like a true professional, went out to deliver arias at 9:00 a.m. on a freezing winter's day, while we were taken through to the area behind the side doors ready for the opening.

As Lesley Garrett finished her songs to rapturous applause, Victoria Beckham was arriving in a splendid horse-drawn carriage. We came out and the photographers went bananas as I handed Kirsty to Victoria, who looked amazing. She was dressed all in white like a Snow Queen; a seductive camisole beneath a trouser suit with a long coat and beautiful white leather gloves. We made so many column inches in the subsequent papers; from Birmingham to Ipswich there were full pictures dedicated to the Hospice cause and us.

Mr Al Fayed's ex-Personal Assistant, Belinda White, and current PA Lisa Escasany were both a joy to know and work alongside, and they both loved calling us with great news. Good news always meant money, whether it came in a one-off amount from Mr Al Fayed himself or from one of the many visitors to the store who, after meeting its owner and seeing Kirsty's picture, signed a cheque before leaving.

It still makes me smile to remember Kirsty, a vulnerable little girl from Northern Moor, opening Harrods' Sale alongside its distinguished owner and the nation's highest profile female celebrity. For Kirsty, the adventure went on.

The Office

After a year I decided I would quite like to have dinner at my own kitchen table, so Philip and I moved our office to Oxford Road, an old knitting shop. The spec, one large room, revolting cellar, kitchen and outside toilet – we know how to live!

Jan and Steve Bruce were refurbishing their home and, luckily for us, they gave us some fabulous office furniture as they were moving house. As BA were relocating to Didsbury, our friend David Preston offered us the opportunity to go to choose some more. I think he was surprised how much we took – including a draughtsman's set of drawers! So we were ready for work.

People imagine that we run a charity from a plush office and we have all the different functions at our command: PR Department, Marketing Department, Creative Department, Volunteer Department, Accounts Department, Human Resources Department – our office is best described as *inhuman resources* as there has only ever been Phil and I and one other person in the office, whether it be Janet, Louise or our very select volunteers, Sue France or Trish Davies. In our office, you have to be all things for all people

We have kept every paper in which Kirsty has appeared, every magazine, every letter that has been sent and we try our very best to acknowledge all donations within a few days. We have crammed into this modest space money-counting machines, lost property, boxes and boxes of wristbands,

Phil and Susie.

badges, toys, tee shirts, CDs, DVDs, all merchandising material for the charity.

The office has of course played host to numerous celebrities – Roy Keane, Gary Pallister, Steve Bruce, Emma Atkins, Samia Ghadie, Bryan Robson – but, most important, we have the royal visit from her ladyship Kirsty. She answers the phones and plays solitaire. Before we gained the services of Tony Dixon, Kirsty's hairdresser, I used to wash her hair in our kitchen sink. To keep the tubes clear she would have to lie on the draining board with her legs kicking the kitchen roll.

Pride of Britain – March 2002

The Pride of Britain Awards celebrate the lives and achievements of remarkable individuals. So the invitation we received in 2002 to be part of it was another great honour for Kirsty.

We were all called to make the official photograph at the ceremony in London, which was to appear in the next day's

Kirsty waves to the Press at the entrance to the Hilton Hotel, Park Lane, London before the Pride of Britain Awards, 5 March 2002. (DM)

Celebrities surround Kirsty at the Pride of Britain Awards. (DM)

Joan Collins meets Kirsty at the Hilton. (DM)

Daily Mirror. Kirsty was placed in the centre on the bottom step and it was wonderful to watch Joan Collins, Cilla Black, Richard Branson and others equally famous crowding around, eager to be pictured next to her!

I charged down between several tables to take Kirsty's oxygen cylinder as Carol Vorderman announced our special little girl. The ramp was not easy to manage and the audience was extremely quiet, but then there was a huge cheer as Kirsty slowly walked to centre stage. For family and friends there is always a little apprehension at moments like these, in case the youngster is overawed, but no-one needed to worry.

'How much money do you need to raise, Kirsty?' asked Carol.

Kirsty dutifully replied 'Fifty million pounds.' The audience fell apart.

Kirsty, Star of Television

Who would have ever believed five years ago when the Appeal began that our little Leading Lady could create enough interest to warrant so much television coverage?

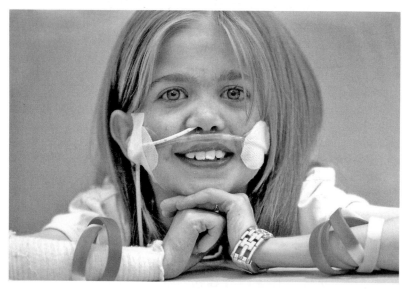

Kirsty with her wristbands.

We graduated from odd slots on digital programmes, to obscure magazine pieces, progressing on to local news and then amazingly the national news. Kirsty has made headlines around the world, culminating in the big one... *Kirsty's Millions*.

After an initial meeting with Paul Stead from Daisybeck Productions, we made a short taster film of Kirsty's story, in an effort to interest a TV company. It worked beyond our dreams, because the BBC commissioned a one-hour documentary. We all wanted something special, taking a sensitive, intimate, 'butterfly on the wall' approach to what would still be a hard-hitting

England rugby star Jonny Wilkinson presents Kirsty with the Helen Rollinson Award, while Gary Lineker looks on, at the Sports Personality of the Year awards, 12 December 2004. (RK BBC PO)

documentary. The team at Daisybeck formed a very special relationship with the staff and the families of the Hospice. Because of their discretion they managed to capture on film real people in real life situations. Anyone who watched *Kirsty's Millions* could not help but understand the necessity of securing lasting funding for children's hospices.

Kirsty's was only one of the stories that featured in the programme but, because of her huge profile, it was Kirsty's story that sold it to the BBC. There was a couple of occasions when we nearly pulled out prior to filming, as I resisted their requests to follow the Howard family's private life because, although Lynn and Steve have always been happy to let Kirsty front the campaign as long as she enjoyed it, they wanted to keep the rest of the family free from intrusion.

Life during that period was totally crazy, because we were still doing all the normal day and night stuff but now we were being filmed doing it. Several months later Paul Stead invited me to see the first cut and, for the first time, I heard Sue Johnston's brilliant voiceover. it was a proud programme, beautifully filmed and produced. Amazingly enough it was screened on the same day as The BBC's Sports Personality of the Year, in which Kirsty already had a starring role, as she was presented with the Helen Rollinson Award for Courage against Adversity.

Trafford Centre

The most difficult part in raising such a large amount of money is keeping up the momentum. The Trafford Centre has played a huge part from 2003–06 in fundraising. After two years of trying to gain help from the Trafford Centre, it was in 2003 that I received a positive call from Kate Holland and, following that, an even more positive meeting. For the first time in the Trafford Centre's history, they had decided to support one cause.

The first element of fundraising was via the beautiful fountains placed here, there and everywhere in the Centre. Half a million footfall per week ensures lots of visitors, especially children, many of whom would love to make a wish and throw in a coin. Not unreasonably all Centres that allow their fountains to be used for fundraising do so on the

The joys of coin-cleaning – left to right: Sue France, Janet Henderson, Susie, Louise Blenkharn and Trish Davies. (TD)

clear understanding that the charity has to clean and count the coins. It is amazing how, from all the volunteers who are very happy to attend the balls and high profile events, there have been only a small core of genuine stalwarts that have stuck with us through that grimy, laborious cleaning of coins: stand up Louise Blenkharn, Sue France, Trish Davies and Janet Henderson!

It is very important at this juncture to make clear how thrilled we were to be the beneficiaries of the Trafford Centre; they have given us enormous help and co-operation and have raised over £100,000 towards our goal. There were numerous events but the biggest by far was to coincide with the Spiderman film launch. It just so happened that we had zillions of Spiderman badges, so the retailers supporting the Trafford Centre fundraising appeal sold them on our behalf and Janet set up her usual conveyer-belt routine, and took charge of all collections.

The big day came and, to draw attention to our spectacular opening, to take place in the afternoon, we persuaded the Trafford Centre window-cleaner to climb up onto the roof

Kirsty with Coronation Street's *Sam Aston, promoting the Spiderman badge launch, 12 July 2004. (MEN)*

dressed as Spiderman. Then Louise, Phil and I rang all the radio stations and newspapers, pretending that we were just members of the general public driving past and saying

'There's a Spiderman on top of the Trafford Centre, do you know why?'

Most people thought it was Fathers for Justice doing their usual sort of stunt but of course, later that day they realised it was 'Children's Hospices for Justice', campaigning for their survival.

There was mass TV coverage. The leading man in a stunning lycra costume abseiled to the sound of the Spiderman theme, and the customers in the Orient gasped as celebrity after celebrity walked on stage. Simon Gregson, although not upstaged, was joined by Spiderman look-alike, Avid Merrion, and a host of celebrities.

Switching on Blackpool lights with Ronan Keating

In the summer of 2002, Kirsty's health had taken a downward spiral and she was referred back to Wythenshawe again, where she was diagnosed with gout. She was transferred to Booth Hall with her knees swollen and her little limbs really struggling to move enough for her to walk.

There have been so many times when Kirsty has been admitted to hospital and each and every such episode remains heart-wrenching, but this particular period was particularly difficult. Gout, being a new complaint for Kirsty requiring different treatment, she had been taken into a different hospital on the other side of Manchester. When I finally found her room she was sitting on her little bed looking extremely lethargic. I took some crazy toys for her but unusually, she did not respond at all; she moaned about the food and was just not happy.

I asked what I could do to make her feel a bit better. What would it take to make a difference? After a little sad-faced pause, she replied 'Ronan Keating'. I should not have been surprised at all as Ronan has always been her favourite pop star and his *I Love You Best When You Say Nothing at All* is Kirsty's song. She has sung her rendition at every occasion we have ever had, in some instances 20 or 30 times in one night! She simply adored both man and song. I told her that for me to succeed in arranging for her to meet Ronan, she would need to be discharged from the hospital so she had to start working on getting better. I then went back to the office and started to phone the Ronan Keating camp.

I learned that Ronan was to switch on the famous lights at Blackpool on Friday 30 August 2002. I got hold of his Management Office, who seemed thrilled at the prospect of involving Kirsty, and said that they would get back to me. I then spoke to the Blackpool organisers of the lights and they were ecstatic at the idea.

It was all going so well until I had a heavy conversation with the producer at Radio 2 who was covering the event; he was not pleased at all. There were some tough exchanges, that made me feel that I might have to give up on the idea, before Mr Producer realised that disappointing such a special child might lead to bad publicity. I admit it was nothing short of emotional blackmail but they changed their minds. Phew – that was a close one!

True to form at 3:00 p.m. on Friday 30 August, Kirsty was discharged and in a taxi on her way to my house. I had the outfit

Kirsty joins Ronan Keating, to switch on the famous Blackpool lights on 30 August 2002. (MEN)

all ready. I washed her hair and got her changed, put a bit of sparkle in her eyes (we girls need a bit of sparkle) and off we went.

Roger the Dodger took us to Blackpool and we arrived on the sea-front, driving through the huge cordoned-off areas to base camp, where the switch-on was to take place. Our timing was impeccable because, as I got out of the car holding Kirsty in my arms, who was the first person we saw ? – Ronan Keating.

He looked at Kirsty and said,

'Are you going to switch these lights on with me?'

Kirsty was in complete and utter shock but managed to reply 'Yes, yes.'

While we awaited our call, the show's whole entourage made their way over to our Winnebago dressing room, to meet Beckham's Angel. The Sugababes were just sweet and lovely, though Kirsty did not know a Sugababe from a jelly babe – she has never been very impressed with females.

We could hear the crowd getting louder and louder, with plenty of screams for Ronan and the others. Darius popped in to say hello while I put some lip-gloss on Kirsty's tiny blue lips. Holding the oxygen, I was led to the side of the stage and sat with Kirsty on my lap as I have done so many times, happy with the feel of her little body, waiting in anticipation for that special moment. Ronan sang, exciting the crowd and building up to the all-important switch-on. Then he proudly introduced Kirsty and I passed her from my arms to his, confident that he would take good care of her. Kirsty was so happy.

They started the countdown and the crowd roared. 10 9 8 7 6 5 4 3 2 (*cue fireworks*) then ONE. We hadn't been warned about the fireworks, so they came as a bit of a shock for Kirsty, but she was exhilarated by the moment and, as the switch-on went over the airwaves and was witnessed in the homes of millions, so she achieved yet another special goal.

Ronan handed her back to me and Kirsty whispered in my ear,

'Oh my God, I'll never sleep tonight for thinking about Ronan Keating.'

The fireworks continued to light up the skies of Blackpool as we travelled in Roger the Dodger's people carrier back to Manchester but, most important, not back to the hospital.

BIRTHDAYS AND ANGEL BALLS

Russell Watson and Kirsty's seventh birthday, Friday 20 September 2002

One day towards the autumn of 2002 I had a message to telephone someone called Perry Hughes. I made the call and this incredibly enthusiastic, excitable character told me that he was Russell Watson's manager and that Russell was interested in making a record in aid of the Kirsty Appeal.

I had met Russell himself several years previously, when our events company was arranging the Ciao Italia Ball, a prestigious gathering to celebrate the restaurateurs of Manchester. It was setting-up time and Phil and I were working on the table names and spacing, when a young man appeared and asked if he could sing that evening. He was a persuasive young man and, once I had listened to him, I realised he would stop the show, for it was the most beautiful sound and delivered with such confidence. That night the standing ovation went on forever and you just knew he was going to be a star.

It was even suggested at one time that I might become Russell's manager so I had been thrilled to see his promise fulfilled as he climbed the ladder over the next years. Now here was an opportunity to have a great operatic star singing for our campaign.

Perry told me that Russell had been working on a song called *Is Nothing Sacred*. He said it was originally intended as a song about love lost but, since seeing Kirsty at the opening ceremony of the Commonwealth Games, each time he and Russell had listened to the song they could not get Kirsty out of their minds. Enthusiasm breeds enthusiasm and, though both our diaries looked full, we managed to meet that very day at the car park of the Belfry House Hotel and by 12:30 I found myself in the passenger seat of Perry's posh car, listening to the song. By the end of the first chorus we both had tears in our eyes. In another ten minutes Perry had

Patron Russell Watson and Coronation Street's *Liz Dawn join Kirsty to celebrate £2milion on 12 March 2003. (MEN)*

phoned Universal Records and we had the first meeting arranged in London.

This was an enormous boost for the Kirsty Appeal. Not only was Russell Watson ready to make a Christmas Song for Kirsty for no fee whatsoever, but he also quickly proved a wonderful ambassador for our cause. In the build-up weeks to our release, he did the tour of Des & Mel, Gloria Hunniford and the rest, speaking glowingly of Kirsty and scathingly of the Government and all the negativity surrounding children's hospices.

It was during this busy run-up to the song's release in December that BKR Haines Watts accountants were due to hold their annual charity ball to support our Appeal and that event coincided with Kirsty's seventh birthday on 20 September. Given the medical prognosis some three years earlier, it always seemed something of a minor miracle when we celebrated Kirsty spending another year among us. So, despite the heavy schedule running up to the record release, Perry Hughes worked wonders to arrange for Russell to come along to the great event and actually meet Kirsty for the first time.

Mere Golf and Country Club was the venue for this birthday ball and Kirsty was resplendent in purple, a beautiful dress made by Sarah at Lucy Lockets. As we sat after dinner at a table which looked through to reception, we saw a door swing open to admit Russell, looking totally immaculate. It really brought home to me what a great career he had forged.

With Russell and Perry came the security guards, holding the biggest parcel you have ever seen, all wrapped in a huge bow. In it was a present I knew Kirsty would love; a massive, sugar pink, Barbie car. After introducing Kirsty, so that everyone could sing *Happy Birthday*, and making my accustomed speech about her and the Appeal, I had the pleasure of inviting Russell to sing. The audience was thrilled and I knew from Kirsty's reaction to Russell that he was definitely going into her top ten list. The cameras flashed, the Barbie car was presented and that was the last we saw of Kirsty's legs that night as she never got out of the car for the rest of the evening. I played Russell's song for the first time and the audience gave its resounding approval, so it was fingers crossed for a Christmas hit for Kirsty.

Angel Ball – 7 December 2002

The week from the 1st to the 7th of December went down without doubt as the busiest, most manic seven days in my life.

Plans for the Angel Ball always begin several months prior to the event but, that year, they were kick-started about eight months before by a phone call from Louis Vuitton, saying that they wanted to help the Kirsty Appeal by having the Ball coincide with the launch of their first branch of Selfridges in Manchester. Can you imagine how exciting that was? I practically somersaulted on my way to the first of an exhausting series of meetings with PR companies, Louis Vuitton local, Louis Vuitton London, structure hire, safety, security and the rest.

I had wanted to use the Lowry Hotel and catering facilities for both events but it was eventually agreed to use a site stage right of the hotel, on some waste ground, with the agreement of the developers who had already bought it. The Louis Vuitton launch would be on Wednesday 4 December and the Third Angel Ball would follow three nights later. This proved to be a big mistake

When Phil and I arrived on Thursday morning immediately after the first event, we found that everything that had made that place special had already been ripped out and was making its way into the nearest lorry. Now, when you consider that the whole thing was sold to us as a fantastic venue for our Angel Ball, just two days away, we had to face the fact that we had a massive problem and were facing potential disaster and a lot of unexpected cost. The star cloth to fill the huge structure, and make it look something like the stunning venue we had promised, alone cost £10,000. Thankfully Louis Vuitton covered the payment. Sleep was out of the question for the next two nights as we worked to rescue the situation with the help of Lin and Jon Pimblett and several others.

Even a few hours before the actual Ball, the heating was not working and, believe me, it was freezing. But *the show must go on* and it did, though unscheduled dramas, like video screens not working, went on as well. The moment that saved it for me personally was when Russell got up to sing. He was spectacular that night; absolutely amazing. Kirsty looked adorable. We were engulfed by celebrities and everyone was completely overawed by the beauty created within our 'fairytale structure'. Rescuing the Ball had cost a lot, but it brought in much more. At £100,000 it was the most we had ever raised at one event, boosted enormously by the fantastic and overwhelming generosity of our celebrities and our audience combined. Not everyone is impressed by the fuss made about people who are famous but, for fundraisers, celebrities often make the difference between success and failure, because everyone likes to say 'Ooooooooh , guess who was there!'. On this night, however, it meant more for us than that. We had whole cast of *Waking the Dead* and, through Sue Johnston, they had offered an auction prize – two people to go along during filming, meet the cast, have lunch and to be in the production as extras.

As Michael Edwards Hammond, who held the auction for us that day, was nearing £10,000 for this lot, Claire Goose came running up to me and said that a business had made a firm commitment to double the amount if we could give the prize twice! So *Waking the Dead* had brought an easy £20,000 towards our target. (When I say 'easy' it certainly seems so in the excitement of a moment of fundraising triumph, although in reality the visits still had to be organised and it was over a year before both parties had claimed their prizes.)

The Ball was a great success, but the days leading up to it had been so horrendous that I think both we and the management of The Lowry couldn't wait to see the back of the marquee.

£2 Million Party – 12 March 2003

Another goal was in sight – a very exciting one at that. We now had £2 million in the bank and we needed a celebration. Looking back, it is amazing to think of all the things that had happened between the £1 million celebration and that day when we celebrated the second. We decided to ask Mike Prophet at the Ambelhurst to support us, and by goodness he did. He organised everything. The makeover for Kirsty was duly arranged and this time it was a fantastic white velvet dress with little pearls.

The national press was still convinced that David Beckham was going to make a surprise appearance. There was a frenzy of photographers waiting hopefully for the end of the speech to introduce Kirsty. The world's newspapers had turned up, the BBC and ITV had brought television cameras and they were all clearly disappointed that their main prey had escaped them, despite all our previous efforts to tell them that he would not be there. However, Russell Watson came and so did our own adorable Liz Dawn.

Kirsty was flabbergasted looking into Liz's face and kept saying,

'I don't believe Vera's here'.

By now she had met many celebrities, but seeing Vera in the flesh was definitely a jaw-dropping experience for little Kirsty. Another of her Coronation Street heroes arrived later in the afternoon; Kevin Kennedy was in his last few months of playing Curly Watts. Kirsty was presented with some lovely gifts that day. Russell bought her a guitar and microphone and Kevin and Kirsty kept us entertained as the guests were beginning to leave.

We all then sat and watched the coverage of the afternoon and it was excellent We made both the evening news programmes and lots of locals but this time the nationals did not bother to carry the story, so there were a lot of wasted man hours for those photographers. It is a strange world that it should not be 'news' when a tiny, terminally ill little girl has raised £2 million pounds and yet it would be news if someone famous drops by for the celebration.

Angel in a Red Dress

Kirsty's Angel Balls have become the most prestigious event in our annual calendar, and the majority of the guests rebook year on year. It has always been very important to make each celebration of Kirsty's birthday unique. The organisation and search for the next year's venue begins almost immediately we close the book on the previous year's. The search for prizes attractive enough to raise a vast amount of money, and the artists who are well-known enough and generous enough to give their services free of charge, the sponsorship, the seating, the table prizes, linen, flowers, lighting and all technical add-ons have all been arranged through our tiny little office and our sensational team of three – Louise, Sue and Janet. On the actual day of the event, we are fortunate to have lots of help from our close friends and, my goodness, by that time the extra hands are needed.

The 2003 Ball was at the Belfry in a Mahood Marquee. As the celebration was Kirsty's actual birthday, she had her very own pantomime and, without any prior knowledge, she was called upon to join the cast and become the Princess. Richard Fleeshman, not then known for his wonderful voice, sang *You Look Wonderful Tonight* to Kirsty. She gazed into his eyes and the entire audience melted, except me!

I was in a high state of excitement waiting for the space beside me to be filled by, wait for it, Hugh Grant. Michael

Edwards Hammond, the auctioneer, was sure that, along with Nicholas Hoult, who starred with Hugh in *About A Boy*, the star was going to join us and also offer a prize for the auction – the rare opportunity to speak a line with Hugh in the next Bridget Jones film. Guess what? He didn't come; in fact he didn't know anything about it!

Thankfully I had not told the press in advance and, luckily for us, the person who paid £7,000 to be an extra was one of our Patrons, Paul Beck – phew!

Since that year each and every Angel Ball and all Kirsty celebrations have featured the most beautiful cakes made and donated by our friends, Lin and Jon Pimblett. These have taken pride of place as they are works of art; fairy castles, carousels, angels – each personalised with exquisite little crystals.

The venue for 2004 was an obvious choice as we had the brand new five-star Radisson Edwardian opening in Manchester and a close friend, Adam Evanson, had now moved from the Radisson SAS (where we had held the Ball in 2002) to the new Manchester venue. Granada TV was making a new series of documentaries called *Big Night Out* and so our efforts to organise this Ball were closely followed by the TV crews. Obviously, when you have a lens pointed at you 24 hours a day it heightens the tension, but they were a small team and good to work with.

As the Ball was being televised, we wanted some special entertainment and, with the help of Russell Watson's ex-manager Perry Hughes, and through the dealings we had with the PR of the record company, we were totally blown away to receive confirmation that Chris De Burgh would attend and entertain for Kirsty. There were no riders; he was as charming as he was talented and the audience lapped up his effortless professionalism. Then he announced:

'Ladies and Gentlemen! We have a very special little girl here this evening and I would like to sing this song for her.'

This obviously sounds as if it had been well-planned and scheduled but in actual fact, Kirsty and I had just rushed up to the bedroom, so that I could change her from her pink ball gown into her red dress.

As the introduction began, Kirsty joined Chris on stage and sat next to him on the piano stool and when he began – *I've never seen you looking so lovely as you did tonight* – there was not a dry eye in the audience. By the end of this Ball, Mark Rix had made his decision to get a *Manchester Evening News* team to climb Mount Kilimanjaro.

A lovely moment in the auction was when one of our patrons, Dr Harold Riley, announced a special auction prize of a little picture of Kirsty together with a poem about her as shown below. In the face of hot competition the final bid went to Chris de Burgh. He took hold of the microphone and said that there was only one place that this picture belonged and that was with her Mum and Dad. That sure was a Big Night Out.

The following poem features Harold's words to accompany Kirsty's portrait.

I remember her in the little garden
behind her house she was tiny but in
spite of her illness she didn't seem frail
her heart was enormous and the charisma
of her being shone out of her
all fathers who have a daughter make
a special bond with their little girl
Kirsty it seems has made a bond with god
to help take the pain away from
other children who are suffering
she is every father's daughter
and god's little angel on earth.

The record – *Is Nothing Sacred Anymore?*

We awoke on Sunday 8 December, exhilarated by the money we had raised, but extremely bleary-eyed after the Angel Ball and the effort of making it happen. Roger arrived with the people-carrier and we headed off to pick up Kirsty, Steve and Lynn from Northern Moor and started off for London because the record launch was scheduled for the very next day.

By now the concierge at the Hyde Park residence in Park Lane knew all the ins and outs of accommodating Kirsty. We made our way once again to one of Mr Al Fayed's stunning

Music legend Chris de Burgh with the little lady in red –
the Angel Ball of 2004 at the Radisson Edwardian, Manchester. (MEN)

apartments, and relaxed for an early night as the morning call was for 8:30 a.m. When you consider the number of things that have to happen as part of a Kirsty makeover, this actually meant a 7 a.m. start at the latest, which is really early for her. As always we were met at entrance door 10 and taken to Mr Al Fayed's private office.

Harrods had provided a beguiling little red velvet dress and Kirsty looked every bit the Christmas sugar-plum fairy.

Almost as soon as we went into the boardroom, cameramen and stills photographers were grabbing shots of Kirsty, our host and Russell. Mr Al Fayed's pipers headed our entourage as we made our way through the Georgian ballroooom to a fabulous set with the Harrods logo, the record's logo and the Kirsty logo.

Even at that early hour there was an exciting buzz in the air, and the room was packed with a crowd of press, TV reporters and fans of Russell and Kirsty. Among the audience was Don Black, the famous writer of so many favourite songs from musical shows, and co-writer on INSAM – I thought to myself, I hope he is going to waive his percentage.

As Russell introduced Kirsty and explained why we were there I saw Nina Nannar and also thought, 'Bloody hell, I hope we get News at Ten again!'

Kirsty – centre stage – full of her own special magnetism. Russell – stage left – and a room full of enthusiastic people. As the backing track began and Russell started to sing, Kirsty never took her eyes off him. What he did not know was that Kirsty had driven us bananas by learning the whole song, which she duly mimed until Russell put the microphone in front of her. Perfectly in tune, she sang along with him. After I had said a few words about the charity and of course expressed my appreciation to Russell and Mr Al Fayed, we moved on to the record department where a huge queue of people was waiting to get Russell's and Kirsty's autographs. The two of them seemed equally popular with the fans but it was marvellous to see Kirsty sitting there, talking to everybody, thinking she was one of the Spice Girls.

Kirsty had always enjoyed the limelight and meeting so many famous people but being so closely involved in an actual record launch was a new treat for her and one made more special by the generosity of the artist involved. When we made the video for the record promotion, Kirsty was more heavily featured than Russell so there was no ego to be massaged there. He showed a full appreciation of Kirsty's own star status and was prepared to go all the way for this song.

Success in the music industry depends on so many factors and nothing is certain. Christmas records in particular are a bit of a lottery; the most promising song may sink like a stone and, as soon as the festivities are over, demand for the record ceases. *Is Nothing Sacred any More* was certainly no disaster, though it never quite made the dizzy heights we thought it deserved. The single got to Number 23, we made £40,000 for the Appeal and gained an awful lot of profile along the way.

The icing on the cake for the song and for all of us was Russell's concert at the *Manchester Evening News* Arena on 21 December when Kirsty was invited to join him as he sang to her. I left Kirsty on the stage and watched her little face on the big screens around the arena. There was a huge ovation, which confirmed the swell of love people felt for Kirsty, while recognising the kindness they saw in the man who had put so much effort into supporting her and her cause.

GREAT MANCHESTER RUNS

In November 2002 I received a phone call from a stranger called David Hart and agreed to meet him, little knowing that we were at the beginning of a great local and national event; an event, furthermore, in which Kirsty and our Appeal would have a major role to play.

David was Communications Director for Nova International and the topic was a ten kilometre run to take place the following May. Kirsty could hardly walk, let alone run, but her presence and profile had kept the Manchester City Council (MCC) supporting our campaign and they had chosen Kirsty's Appeal as the nominated charity for the Great Manchester Run. But of course there was an implicit *quid pro quo*. As in everything to do with fundraising, you 'don't get owt for nowt' and David was keen to tap into our celebrity contact database.

The meeting room overlooked Albert Square and it was bland and cold, but running off the back of the enormous success of the Commonwealth Games and also my background in the earlier Piccadilly Radio marathons, David's words sparked my enthusiasm and we soon shared the same vision.

Seeing enormous possibilities, I met with Russ Vine and his team at Cheetham Bell and discussed how we could promote the run. The main point was to recruit as many runners as possible, while convincing people this could be fun. We decided we needed a TV ad to achieve maximum exposure but had no money to make one; so we had to find it. LBM generously agreed and Cheetham Bell recruited the team that would make the ad for next to nothing.

We all agreed our first choice to star in the advert would be the very popular Charity Dingle from *Emmerdale* (Emma Atkins). Emma agreed straight away and we had to recruit two others to co-star as a pantomime horse. We were blatantly copying the Nike advert, where the 'bus splashes the runners. I have known Anthony Prophet since he was five, he adored Kirsty, and when I asked him if he wanted to star in a TV advert for her he was overwhelmed... for about two seconds, until he realised that he would be the back part of a pantomime horse. Oh and could he possibly recruit the front half as well?! This part went to Ged Hall.

Filming took place in the centre of Manchester and the streets were cleared of traffic. The director was shouting through his megaphone – ACTION. You would have to see the ad to believe it, but Emma, Anthony and the whole crew worked until dusk, ending up on location in a park in Prestwich where poor Emma and the boys were shattered; wet, dirty but exhilarated.

Even with the ad, we didn't have the infrastructure to manage either the runners or the sponsorship on such a huge scale but, with us handling the press build-up and the fact that we were able to bring on board Bryan Robson, Samia Ghadie, the Chief Constable of Manchester, Mike Todd, and many more to promote a run that was then unknown, Nova was highly delighted to find it had 10,000 runners.

Stars of Emmerdale *support Kirsty at the Great Manchester Run of 26 May 2003 – left to right: Jeff Hordley, Charlotte Belling, Emma Atkins, and Tony Audenshaw. (MEN)*

First Great Manchester Run – Monday 26 May 2003

For the night before this first run, David had booked us into the Jury's Inn, where many of the athletes were also staying. As they arrived, a disabled athlete pointed out that Kirsty's cumbersome wheelchair was far from adequate to take part in something like this. I felt really embarrassed and made a mental note; must get turbo-charged, designer, streamlined wheelchair with go faster stripes for next year – pale pink if possible.

The weather was beautiful for the Bank Holiday and Kirsty was delivered to my door for the normal makeover. I had all her running gear placed out on the bed. She was a bit grumpy, as always first thing in the morning but, after a couple of sausages and a cup of tea, we left to make our way with David Hart, who was well enamoured with Kirsty by now, to the starting point. The atmosphere in Manchester that day was electrifying. The juniors lined up and the compère was telling the eager crowd all about Kirsty. But, when the starting pistol went off, hundreds of children zoomed past, leaving Kirsty in her old-fashioned low-tech wheelchair to come last in the race.

That first year, the ending of the 10 km senior race was killing, as it was uphill entering GMEX. Everyone was knackered and the cameras caught those pained expressions but, on reaching the finishing line, who was in front of the crowd to cheer all the runners? Kirsty.

Bryan Robson has probably still not forgiven me for his swollen knee, although I did do my best with ice cubes. Steve Bruce joined Bryan for the TV interviews, along with Samia Ghadie and from *Emmerdale* – Emma Atkins, Charlotte Bellamy, Tony Audenshaw, Chris Chittel, and Jeff Hordley.

This was a huge success for Manchester, huge profile for the run and for the Appeal, but must do better next year.

The Second Run

Next year came soon enough and I was determined this time to make some money for the Appeal. My meetings with David started in the November. David spoke to Vicki Rosin from MCC and made sure they were going to continue to support us. This

Peter Schmeichel, Kirsty and Coronation Street's *canine Schmeichel start the 2004 Great Manchester Run. (MEN)*

meant that when applications came in with Kirsty's box ticked, Janet could add them to the database.

I also arranged a meeting with Alan Grant at NTL, along with a representative from NOVA, to discuss sponsorship.

It seemed perfect. NTL was going to sponsor the Kirsty Appeal on the run and we would receive tee-shirts for all our runners; but the reality turned out far from what we intended. NTL part-sponsored the actual race and the money we thought would be for us was swallowed up in the main sponsorship deal – so guess what? No tee-shirts again. So after words with David Hart, NOVA themselves agreed to supply tee-shirts for our runners. It was a good job it did not rain that day as it would have turned into the biggest see-through, wet tee-shirt competition Manchester has ever known.

Janet, our secretary, applied her usual common sense and got us all placed in a production line to fold tee-shirts, print sponsorship forms, stuff envelopes, add labels, stick stamps, cut fingers... paper cuts hurt , we know, thanks Janet!

Meanwhile David Hart's appetite for celebrities had not slackened. After last year he and his office had named me the celebrity thief so I wasn't about to prove him wrong.

At that time *Coronation Street's* canine star was Schmeichel, a Great Dane. The stunning acting qualities of little Sam Aston as Chesney were heightened by the casting of this beautiful dog. I had known Peter Schmeichel, the goalkeeper, for many years and my instinct for a great PR story was to bring together Schmeichel the man and Schmeichel the dog, making *Two Great Danes.* Peter agreed and then came a first for me, approaching a dog agent! It took one phone call and a great press story awaited. David Hart was satisfied for another day.

Day-to-day events were being filmed for the BBC's documentary, *Kirsty's Millions*, and so the morning of the race was even more terrifying. Louise stayed with me at the hotel the

Kirsty holds hands with her very grown-up boyfriend Richard Bowden, whom she first met at the £1million celebration – here at the Great Manchester Run in 2004. (MEN)

day before and Phil arrived as dawn broke. Kirsty and I went through the same routine as last year but there were numerous issues that Phil and Louise had to sort out because of the usual jobsworths. Schmeichel the dog was stuck on the other side of the City centre without a VIP entrance badge, so they would not let him through the barriers!

Kirsty, meanwhile, had a headache and was only looking forward to seeing the dog. Then Peter Schmeichel's taxi failed to turn up. There was a lot of shouting and arm-waving from Louise and Philip till eventually things slipped into place and Kirsty, in her new fancy wheelchair and again wearing 'Number 1', waited for the lift doors to open and the four-legged Schmeichel to emerge.

The Great Dane emerged to a great flashing of cameras and he was so enormous that Kirsty was a little apprehensive; he was much bigger in real life than he seemed on a television screen. We made our way to the starting line and met up with Peter and Bente, his wife. The 'two Schmeichels' and Kirsty posed for what was a front-page story before the race itself had even begun.

Kirsty's number one boyfriend, Richard Bowden, ran alongside her down the cobbles on Coronation Street. But, God bless her, even with the new wheelchair she still came last.

It takes forever for people to collect the sponsorship, but we knew within six weeks, that this was definitely going to be a major fundraising event.

The Third Run

By its third year the Great Manchester Run (GMR) had become literally a runaway success. NOVA could not keep up with the overwhelming interest and had to close the applications. This was the year when they decided to separate the junior from the senior race.

Kirsty had become used to being at the centre of the event and her excitement at wearing the much coveted 'Number 1' started to grow many months before the race. She actually counts down the days to significant dates like these, as she also does for her birthdays.

Kirsty doing what she does so well – promoting the Appeal with a radiant smile and a mature confidence, at the production of Toystory *at the* Manchester Evening News *Arena. (MEN)*

Kirsty talks to Prime Minister Tony Blair at 10 Downing Street in February 2001. (MS P)

ABOVE: Victoria Beckham holds Kirsty at the 2001 Angel Ball, at the Radisson SAS, Manchester Airport (MEN) while BELOW: Kirsty flirts with her husband at the Lowry Hotel four years later. (CG MEN)

The stars of Emmerdale *support Kirsty in the Great Manchester Run of May 2003 – left to right: Jeff Hordley, Charlotte Belling, Emma Atkins and Tony Audenshaw. (MEN)*

ABOVE: Kirsty and Susie celebrate £3 million at the Circle Club in Manchester on 10 November 2004, joined BELOW: by an array of celebrities, to celebrate another £ million a year later at the MICC, G Mex, Manchester Angel Ball. (Both MEN)

Jonny Wilkinson presnts Kirsty with the Helen Rollinson Award at the Sports Personality of the Year 12 December 2004. (RK BBC PO)

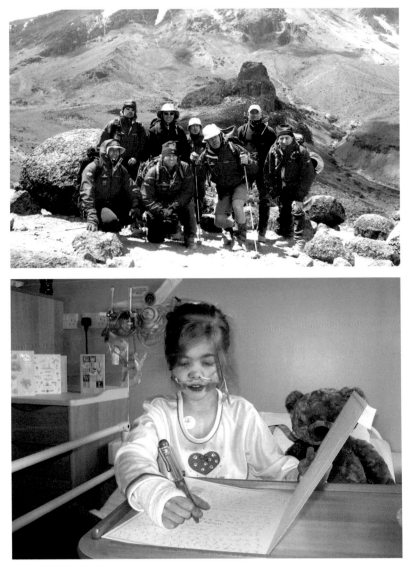

ABOVE: The Manchester Evening News *team at the summit of Mt Kilimanjaro in August 2005 – left to right: Mark Rix, Paul Horrocks, Phil Davenport, Dave Healey, Hervey Magnall, Phil Tonge, Ian Marshall and Dave Rix. (MEN) BELOW: Kirsty recovers in hospital after her relapse in July 2005. (SM for MEN)*

Kirsty – Angel of Courage. (YFA)

The Sue Johnston whom I had known for many years was by this time a national celebrity. She had won the Comedy Actress of the Year and the accolades for her success in *Waking The Dead* and *The Royle Family* had elevated her to stardom. After a few drinks one night, Sue agreed to run the Great Manchester Run, despite the fact that she did not even possess a pair of trainers. The plan was that she would train methodically to build her strength up for the race – with her work schedule she could scarcely fit in a jog, let alone build up to 10 K training runs. Phil and I plotted how, if she was exhausted, he might surreptitiously remove her from the throng and place her at the end for the photo calls. Oh ye of little faith! – Sue was triumphant. Phil ran alongside her with his very full English breakfast, a few Silk Cuts, and a raging hangover. The two of them romped to the finish line. There was no prouder supporter that day than Sue's son Joel, watching with Louise and me from the viewing rostrum.

Looking back on the Junior race which, for the first time, took place at the Manchester City Stadium, we were thrilled to have the support of *Coronation Street*'s new star Antony Cotton, whose role turned out to be greater than he was expecting. As the crowd waited for Kirsty to take her place, proudly wearing her 'Number 1' presented to her this year by David Beckham, disaster struck! The wheelchair motor blew up. In all these years, there have been very few occasions that I have seen Kirsty cry, but on this occasion she was devastated. Everyone tried to reconnect the wires but to no avail. Fabulous Antony Cotton and Philip pushed her round the whole course so this time Kirsty wasn't last!

The Fourth Run

By the time we were planning GMR4, David Hart was fully aware that we had established a relationship with Andrew 'Freddie' Flintoff so, not surprisingly, he was looking for Freddie to start the race. Of course, that is exactly what I wanted as well, but I was so aware of his busy schedule and he had already committed support through his benefit year. I had written to him but, with his match commitments and his extraordinary, high-profile year, I fully understood that he

David Beckham and Kirsty at the third Great Manchester Run

David Beckham makes Kirsty laugh at the launch of the
Great Manchester Run of 2005. (CG MEN)

Cricket legend Freddie Flintoff joins Kirsty's helpers at the 2006 Great Manchester Run – left to right: Jan Plant, Carrie Picaethly, Trish Davies, Freddie, Louise Blenkharn and Jenny Markey. (NI)

had not had time to reply. Every other day, I would get a text or an e-mail from David and meanwhile put in place several back-up plans.

I had firm commitments from many of the *Coronation Street* stars, including Antony Cotton, who was progressing from the Junior to the Big Boys race this year and had even been training. Then once again, disaster struck. Owing to the wedding date of one of the cast members, the annual soap awards were rescheduled to film the night before the Great Manchester Run and of course they are filmed in London. There was no way I could expect Antony, Samia and their friends not to enjoy the soap stars' biggest night. They were all up for individual awards, so we were back to an uncomfortably bare drawing board.

At the eleventh hour, Freddie came up trumps for us and agreed to start the Senior Race. We had succeeded once again in bringing the sporting hero of the year to open the GMR! Owing to its growing popularity, there were now a whopping 25,000 participants and I had expected Freddie just to start the first two phases of the race, but instead he left the podium to join the runners on the road. Our other rescuer was Kerry Katona. Though Freddie had agreed to play his part, the loss of our *Coronation Street* friends had deprived us of a celebrity to make the local news and television; it is really important to find someone willing and able to talk about the Appeal.

Suddenly I thought of Kerry; I had written previously through her management company to ask for her support but most management companies, seeing no commission in charity work, do not bother to reply to such approaches. I felt there was a chance of making contact as Kerry lived locally, and I remembered seeing on local news programmes that she had started a local taxi firm for women only. So I rang the Company, asked if they could get a message through to Kerry and left my phone number. I could not believe it – within 10 minutes she rang. I asked her to start the Junior race and, once she had looked at the next couple of days' commitments, she rang back and said that wonderful word – YES!

The previous three years, the GMR had been blessed by the most beautiful weather. We had loved watching from our Jury Inn bedroom window as Manchester came alive in the build-up to the race. The cars are stopped at 6:30 a.m. so the route can be prepared, the barriers appear, the men in yellow seem to swarm at around 7:30 a.m. and, as the excitement builds, the sun has grown stronger.

The rain was torrential. This was the first year we had high-quality tee-shirts, sponsored by Joe Bloggs, but children and adults alike had to cover themselves, and our logo!, in bin bags in a vain attempt to keep dry. There must be a God because, when Kirsty came out to take her place with Kerry, the rain just stopped.

For me, the excitement of the GMR was greater when the Junior and the Senior race took place on the same day. I never felt that the separation worked and there has never been quite the same atmosphere. Yet Kirsty was cheered regardless and Kerry struck up an immediate empathy with her.

As in every other year, our compact, fantastic team all made their way back to Jury's Bar, awaiting our little star Kirsty.

Those were lovely times, reflecting on the race and appreciating the enormity of the love and support from the spectators.

Unfortunately we knew that this would be the last time we would be involved in quite this way. Since our target was in sight, I knew that this would be our final Great Manchester Run for the Kirsty Appeal. But even though the Kirsty Appeal was coming to a close, it was fundamental that Manchester City Council realised that the Hospice needed their continuing support so, after the initial pre-run meetings this year, David Hart arranged to bring Vicki Rosin from MCC to see Francis House. Vicki, through David, had supported us tremendously, even running the race for us herself; this year, her daughter and her friends were going to be taking part in the Junior Run. The ticks on the application form for the Kirsty Appeal were thanks to them both, but it was important that Vicki visited the Hospice and recognised that the support of the Council would still be needed.

Long may the Great Manchester Run continue and, although I am relieved not to have to be its celebrity thief anymore, I am so proud of Manchester, the Great Manchester Run and most of all of what Kirsty has achieved.

ALARMS AND EXCURSIONS

Facing Mortality: I didn't plan for this

Thursday 23 December 2004 seemed a dull, routine kind of day until the moment in the late afternoon when I discovered a lump in my left breast. Panic set in and I immediately made an appointment at my doctor's surgery before asking my friend and neighbour to make quite sure that the lump really existed. It did.

The hours seemed endless until the morning of Christmas Eve when I reached the West Timperley Medical Centre. Sadly my doctor, John Vincent, whom I admire and trust, was not available so I was examined by a locum who was very nice and very pregnant.

'It could be fine but please phone today, and make an appointment with a breast surgeon.'

My Christmas Eves have been the same for many years. Collect the turkey or goose from Kirks Butchers in Styal, Cheshire, then go to see Sister Aloysius at the Hospice, exchanging our gifts whilst sipping sherry, and finally to Kirsty's home to deliver her presents. Although I was making the same moves, the Christmas songs on the radio unnerved me. I was feeling petrified. I rang BUPA at Whalley Range for the first available appointment, which of course was after Christmas, Monday the 29th

Several years prior to this I had helped to set up an Appeal for breast cancer, which we christened Genesis. I tried to contact the marvellous surgeon who instigated the charity, Dr Lester Barr, but he was on holiday with his family, so I was to see a Professor Nigel Bundred.

Nothing prepares you for the heart-stopping moment when you hear the words that change your life forever. Even whilst going through further investigations I held my breath as I asked

'So do I have breast cancer?'

There was a very short pause before the Prof said

'Yes, a malignant tumour.'

My first reaction was to ask if the operation could take place there and then. Get it out quick! But Professor Bundred's advice was to leave it a few days so I could come to terms with what was happening. There are times when not having a Mum really matters, and this was certainly one of them. However, I phoned my friend and neighbour, Sue, and adoptive parents Joan and Neil Cliffe, and they arrived to comfort me.

New Year's Eve was a very strange affair. Sue and I have shared many of them, always saying 'Will we still be on our own next year?' Still stranger for me was Sue's Northern 60th Birthday Celebration, which Phil and I had arranged for Saturday 3 January, the day before I was to be in hospital. When the party was in full swing I looked around the room at so many friends, who seemed to be moving in slow motion.

'Will I ever see them again?' I thought 'Blimey, if you have to be positive about this situation, then I'm done for!'

The 'what's it all about' syndrome hit heavy, closely followed by the thought 'Oh well, if I should die I can have no complaints. I've lived a life full to overflowing: three husbands and three careers, so stop feeling sorry for yourself!'

Then I thought about Kirsty. She had only lived for seven years and most of them in hospital – she is far braver than me.

Sunday came soon enough and, after a surprise visit from Steve and Jan Bruce, I found that Sue had invited more of our friends and she cooked one of her usual amazing, all-singing-and-dancing Sunday lunches. As we sat down to enjoy Sue's feast, I joked that it was like The Last Supper but no one laughed!

Sue drove me to the Hospital that Sunday evening and then returned first thing in the morning to be with me as I was taken to the operating theatre. I have spent many years of my life in theatres but this was a performance out of my control. When I opened my eyes in the recovery room, Sue was there again. She said that, as I regained consciousness, I gave a barrage of abuse. Oh thank goodness I'm alive!

It turned out that there were two tumours and I had the lymph glands removed from my left arm to protect me from the spread of cancer cells. It was a long four days waiting to find out whether the cancer had spread but on Friday, the ninth day of the New Year, the Prof (who by now I called Nigel) arrived smiling (good sign!) to tell me that the prognosis was good. Philip was on his multi-text immediately – yippee, she's going to be fine. But mentally I felt anything but fine. For the first time in my life I was not in control. Even through the darkest years I had always simply got on with life.

The next hurdle of the treatment left me flailing miserably. My oncologist, Dr Alan Stewart, realised that I was breaking down and re-admitted me to hospital for psychiatric care. I felt so alone. Sue was in London and my adoptive parents were not in good health. I thought the pain would go if I just couldn't feel any more.

Then one day I opened my eyes to see Sister Aloysius at my bedside and she gave me the hope and inspiration which led me back onto the path to Kirsty.

I started to focus on the Campaign and I knew that I needed to reach the target of £5 million for all of us. I had made a promise five years ago to the Committee – Sister Aloysius, Father Tom Mulheran, David Ireland and Ged Cosgrove – that, if it were the last thing I would do, I would raise the money to secure the Hospice: and I knew I wanted to be with Kirsty at the end.

Kirsty was not aware of my illness, and of that I am glad, but I really missed her in my days of recovery. I haven't been blessed enough to conceive even with the help of the test tube pioneer Patrick Steptoe, so Kirsty is the closest I have ever been to any child.

Philip had taken charge of the office and I had every faith in him, but I had to have a goal of my own at that time as I felt the Appeal slipping away from me, so I picked up my broken spirit and got back in the race.

Kirsty's Mediterranean Adventure
Outward bound, Phil Taylor writes:

'Island Cruises decided to support the appeal for 2004 and offered Kirsty and her family a Mediterranean cruise. Realising instantly that Kirsty could not fly I knew I would have to drive her to France. I decided Susie would not be well enough after her treatment for a long drive so arranged for the family to fly with Susie, while Louise would join me on the trip with Kirsty and her mum.

'Friday 13 August
'When the day came Louise, Kirsty, Lynn and I set off in Kirsty's favourite car Sally Doolally, (Kirsty named it on account of the sat nav system). I had planned on two days travelling but I was still panicking that if the oxygen was not delivered in France, we would not have enough to travel back. As it was the car was fit to burst, loaded up with ten 45lb oxygen cylinders, two concentrators, a large bag of medicines, a huge box of the drip feeds, a bag of extension tubes for the oxygen, and a suitcase.

'We were all very excited, setting off on an adventure that we had never dreamed possible. Thinking a journey of this magnitude for an eight-year-old little girl would be daunting, I expected Kirsty to get bored along the way but she never complained once or asked "how far to go?". She always looked to Sally, which displays the miles and hours left. But woe betide the sat nav on a long stretch of motorway if she did not speak – Kirsty would shout 'Wake up Sally'. Kirsty entertained us with her wit, charm and, of course, cheek and her ability to invent her own games, played by her rules, and always in her favour!

'Reaching Calais, there were 868 miles and 13 hours to go! Kirsty read the *Famous Five* to her mum and the card cheating continued throughout the trip.

'On our first night I discovered the only missing piece of equipment that none of us had thought of – a continental adapter plug to set the concentrator up. Luckily Louise found one at the hotel and, as we were all tired, we ate and slept in preparation for our next day of travelling.

'The only time Kirsty slept was for thirty minutes on the final leg of the journey. We were all bored without her to entertain us and couldn't wait for her to wake so Louise could continue to play secretaries and for the general banter.

'We checked in and were all glad to be able to go for a walk and get some normal food. On Sunday we were to be collected at midday to be transferred to the ship in Toulon.

'At the ship we were greeted by Captain John O'Neil. I went on board first to check the oxygen and concentrators had been delivered and to choose a cabin for Kirsty and her parents. For me this was also a personal journey. Having always tended to keep my emotions protected in relation to Kirsty, these two days changed everything. She had now stolen my heart. '

We rejoined Kirsty, Lynn and Phil at the ship. Steve and the girls were really looking forward to seeing Kirsty and to start enjoying their very first holiday abroad. We had a meeting with the entire team and then we were led to our cabins. Although this was going to be a journey for the Howard family to enjoy, there was an element of work for Kirsty and myself. The sailaway party was fantastic. We joined the Captain on the bridge as we left the port. There was champagne and all the guests on board were thrilled to know that Kirsty was travelling with them.

Five out of the seven evenings, Kirsty and I were escorted by cruise director Alex, to give little speeches to the guests and also, more important, to the staff. Island Cruises arranged for *The Kirsty Story* to be shown on every cabin's TV and, if she was not known at the beginning of the journey, she was famous by the end.

Kirsty's appetite, which had always been a problem, suddenly was not – it was so good and varied she actually put on weight.

Each morning, as we docked in a different country, we were all woken by the anything-but-dulcet tones of the Captain, telling us what we could and could not do, the times of the excursions and the timings for departure. It was a huge rigmarole to take Kirsty off the ship but, with the help of Marcy, the Guest Relations Manager, two private excursions were arranged. One was to Rome, the Vatican city, that meant very little to Kirsty. We showed her the wonderful statues and, as we made our way out of St Peter's Basilica into the square, Kirsty exclaimed 'Oh look, they've copied the Trafford Centre!'

By this time my legs were giving way and Kirsty let me share her wheelchair. If we stopped for more than a minute on the road, people thought we were begging. As we neared the Trevi fountain, we were guided by two dodgy Roman soldiers, who looked as if their costumes were made of Brillo pads. Kirsty had her photograph taken continually and then she sat on the edge of the most famous fountain in the world; thank God we didn't have to clean the coins for that one! I would like to record here that my most vivid memory of Rome will always be the wish Kirsty made that day. Just imagine: tiny Kirsty, full of excitement and expectation, the sound of the fountain and the splendour of the architecture and Kirsty's wish was profound 'I wish that I could have a baby.'.

Curiously Kirsty's most vivid memory of that day was when Phil had his mobile phone stolen whilst we were eating lunch. Goodness knows why but she thought it was hysterical.

One of the many worries prior to the cruise was how Kirsty could deal with sea sickness. We need not have worried. Whilst every one of us was either petrified or being sick or, like Steve, walking the decks on the night of the biggest storm and rolling seas – Kirsty slept right through it all.

The days when we were in port, but did not disembark, were actually very pleasurable as we had more room to swim and sunbathe and use the facilities.

When we arrived in Ajaccio, Corsica it was a beautiful morning and Marcy had arranged for the Captain and his family to join us to visit the seaside. Kirsty's experience of seeing sand, buckets and spades and all the things that many children take for granted is non-existent. As we arrived at this pleasant cove, one tiny café and a huge stretch of soft sand, it was the perfect picture postcard.

Oxygen wheels don't revolve that well on sand, so Steve was doing his he-man act until we found a place to settle. Meanwhile Louise, Zoe and Kim just stripped off and ran into the sea and the three of them were jumping the waves, which were huge. Kirsty prised herself away from cuddling Alex because she was so determined to join her sisters and jump the waves. Everybody got into action stations to organise her tubes and extension lead to enable her to reach them.

Calamity struck; once everything was in place, the oxygen was not reaching our little one. As Steve quickly put the oxygen back on a short lead to enable her to breathe properly, she became quite devastated and broke down into uncontrollable tears but Alex put on his Superman suit – he certainly did in Kirsty's eyes – and began straightening out all the leads. We all had the same aim and that was to make sure that Kirsty at least put her toes in the sea.

So Kirsty had her wish and, with a little poetic licence, can be said to have jumped the waves. Actually these were huge and there was no way that Kirsty's little body could withstand the force and power; she had to be held there The men all lined up to take turns – Phil, Alex and the Captain, whilst the rest of us got so much pleasure from watching her happy, expressive face. It was sheer delight!

That whole visit was so enjoyable that even the Captain was late back to the ship that day.

Anyone who goes on a cruise wants to have dinner with the Captain. Kirsty, having already nicked his cabin, was the belle of the ball at the Captain's table. Looking back, those seven days were very special. I have always thought it is all about striving to raise money for charity *and* having a good time doing it.

Kirsty takes a break from her cruise, to pray at the
Trevi Fountain in Rome. (LB)

Return – Phil Taylor Writes:

'Sally was set and we drove away from the ship, waving goodbye – all crying. Luckily, everyone had gone back on board straight away and no-one saw that we had driven past that ship four times before finding our way out of the port.

'Kirsty and Alex had been singing one favourite song throughout the whole holiday and it only took twenty minutes into the journey before her little voice chirped up *I am Sailing* over and over and over again. I had to threaten to throw her out of the window if she did not shut up – so she sang it louder than ever.

'Approaching Paris, I thought a little cultural education might be in order, so I pointed out the Eiffel Tower. Kirsty gave it the slightest of glances and replied, "Do you mind? – I am playing cards!"

'We arrived back in England early and joined the M25. Five hours later we were still there. It got so bad that the petrol was low but, more important, so was Kirsty's oxygen and we were stuck in the outside lane. Louise used her charms to stop the traffic in the other two lanes and we had to drive along the hard shoulder to get off the motorway to change the cylinder and find a petrol station.

'We arrived back in Manchester safely around the same time as the rest of the party, who had flown home, and we dropped Lynn off at Gala Bingo! Louise and I travelled back to my home, missing Kirsty already, but knowing our lives had been enriched by our extraordinary adventure.

THE FINAL COUNTDOWN

Angel Ball 2005 – We reach £4m

Oooh – where shall we go this year? The guest numbers are growing but sadly the venues in Manchester are not. I was looking at the possibilities of GMEX and arranged a visit through an old friend of mine, Karen Monks who, through her job with the Bird Consultancy, arranged the PR. We met the manager, David Mallard, and talked over the possibilities of such a large venue. I explained that the appeal would never put down huge deposits and David suggested using the Manchester International Convention Centre (MICC). It was a vast space and for our one day would need a huge amount of people and equipment to make it work. It would also have to be efficiently managed as there was only an overnight and day to prepare.

It seemed a near-impossible task but Dave and Karen both realised that the publicity would raise the profile of their

The celebrities congratulate Kirsty on reaching £4 million at the 2005 Angel Ball, at the MICC, G Mex, Manchester. (MEN)

Lord Jeffrey Archer presides over the auction at the Angel Ball in 2005.
(MEN)

splendid but underused venue. They were prepared to go beyond anything I had ever expected, to accommodate the 2005 Ball. Nevertheless, when Louise and I arrived on the day, the sight that greeted us made our St Tropez tans, sprayed on the day before, melt into a dirty, lined mess.

The usual suspects arrived, trying to keep out of the way from cranes, lighting equipment, staging and whatever as the deliveries began to arrive. A heavily pregnant Esther, a friend from the *Evening News*, had arranged the free use of seat covers and all 700 of them arrived, so Janet arranged the conveyer belt system again.

Four hundred chairs later, we realise the chair covers are two different colours. We can't push the tables forward, stage is not erected, we can't set tables as dance floor's not down, we can't finish lighting because the wheels on the crane need to go on the dance floor. Bloody Hell!

We were nowhere near ready for our artists' rehearsals and still had all the tables to set with the pledge envelopes, the brochures, the prizes, the pencils and the table names The time was racing by, but the staff was not. Panic was beginning to set in and, once again, the whole build-up was being televised. Whatever the chaos on a day like this, there had to be a cut-off point because, when Kirsty arrived, I needed to start the routine of getting her ready and prepared for her most special night.

By the time the rehearsals for Jon Christos began, the producer of the Granada Kilimanjaro documentary, Sian, wanted to interview me. I was so stressed I was stuttering and I could hardly find time to welcome Hayley Westenra who Perry Hughes had arranged to join the evening's entertainment.

Somehow Phil and Louise, helped by Trish, Sue, Janet and Jenny, tied up all the loose ends and arranged and set all the prizes in an amazingly short time. This left them with only fifteen minutes to get themselves ready for the evening but thanks to their efforts, by the time the first guests entered the room, the MICC looked a stunning venue for Kirsty's Angel Ball.

The Manchester Evening News *team at the summit of Mt Kilimanjaro – left to right: Mark Rix, Paul Horrocks, Phil Davenport, Dave Healey, Hervey Magnall, Phil Tonge, Ian Marshall and Dave Rix, August 2005.*
(MEN)

As well as being our annual celebration, the Ball marked the countdown to reaching £4 million. As always, the biggest fundraising part of the evening was the auction and this year we were certainly blessed. Our auctioneer (arranged through one of our patrons, Paul Beck) was Lord Jeffrey Archer, who triumphantly overcame being 'gunged' at the entrance, to give a performance par excellence. And the prizes were spectacular!

One of our very special guests of the evening was Freddie Flintoff, triumphant from England's Ashes victory, who had confirmed he would be in attendance. Freddie joined Lord Archer to assist with auctioning the signed England bat and then, on the spur of the moment, decided to donate the actual bat that he used to gain the final runs at Trent Bridge. Those two items alone raised £33,500 and, when we celebrated reaching our £4 million, Kirsty cried with joy and Freddie himself broke down in tears at meeting her.

Our Last Angel Ball for 2006 will be held at the new Hilton Hotel on Deansgate in Manchester, where we will continue the celebration minus the incorrect chair covers and the panic.

Kirsty's Relapse

'Kirsty's dead.' Those were the words Sue said to me as I opened the door of Poulton Golf Club. I fell to the ground carrying Sue with me. We were slumped in a state of disbelief, screaming and crying. The memories of the moments that followed still leave me feeling icy cold; I love her so that I felt as though I had lost my baby.

Since the beginning of the Appeal I have always had my mobile phone switched on 24 hours a day, not for the numerous calls regarding the fundraising that interrupt us in unsocial hours, as they do in *E.R.*, but because of Kirsty herself and the constant worry about her wellbeing. But on this occasion I was rushing, arriving from the office and walking along the water's edge from my home to the golf club with its marquee erected ready to house Sue's guests, celebrating her Mum's 90th birthday, an event we were organising the following day.

Phil, after dropping off some candelabras at the marquee, had popped in for a drink with Louise at the Chetwode Arms. It was a normal Friday evening until 7:01 p.m., when Phil's mobile rang with the call from Kirsty's dad, Steve.

'Hi Steve.'

'Kirsty's dead.

'WHAT?'

'What did I just say?'

'I'll call you back.'

Phil put the phone down in total shock and told Louise about the short, sharp conversation.

What had happened in Steve's own words was this:

'On 29 July 2005 Kirsty was admitted to hospital suffering this time from, of all things, gout. We are so used to life in hospital, it was just the same routine. Lynn, who always stays overnight, had gone home to change her clothes and I was sat talking to Kirsty who was eating some Skittles. Kirsty then went very quiet. *Please don't let this be the moment I was dreading*, but it was. I nudged her but got no response. I then knew it was a cardiac arrest. Even though Kirsty's eyes were open, I knew she was dead.

'I ran out of the room, I called after the nurse, the urgency in my voice left no doubt – *"Jeanette, I need you... NOW"*. She hit the alarm and immediately started to do CPR on Kirsty. Within minutes the crash team arrived and I was panicking as I couldn't get hold of Lynn; she doesn't drive and I wanted my wife there.

'Our home is only a short distance away so there weren't that many lights to go through on red! Lynn and I were back at Wythenshawe, looking on helplessly at the doctors and nurses trying to resuscitate our little girl.

'For the next couple of hours it was touch and go and our hopes were fading. We were then told that Kirsty's condition had stabilised and they were moving her to Pendlebury Children's Hospital because it specialises in children with heart problems. To do this they had to bring all the equipment from Salford to Wythenshawe and slowly had to swap all the equipment on Kirsty and then re-stabilise her.

'Lynn stayed with Kirsty in the ambulance and I drove over there with Zoe and Kim, Kirsty's sisters. Hours went by, which was really scary and then Kirsty went for a CAT scan and we held our breath until we thankfully found out that there was no brain damage. By Saturday afternoon Kirsty was taken off the life support machine and was breathing on her own. Thank God.'

After Steve's initial call, Phil and Louise had left the Chetwode immediately and headed for Cinnamon Brow where I live, frantically making phone calls on the way in an effort to get hold of me. They decided to contact Sue direct but her answerphone as always took the call and went to speakerphone. Louise screamed 'Sue, Joel, please pick up the phone, it's urgent!' and the panic in her voice was enough to ensure that they did. Phil was so shocked that all he could manage to say to Sue was 'Steve phoned, Kirsty has died, get Susie, we are on our way'.

Phil and Louise live only 20 minutes away, but it seemed a long journey as they drove while still trying to get back to Steve on the mobile. They had a couple of miles left to go when Steve called back.

'They're trying to resuscitate her!!'

Steve told Phil there were five doctors and three nurses working on Kirsty's little body, trying to bring her back to life. She was responding, yet only slightly. There was just a four percent chance of her surviving. Four percent! Although four percent is very small, it was four percent more than 20 minutes previously.

As we made our way to Sue's, she reminded me that special friends were going to be arriving from London to stay at my house for Margaret's party. Then Philip arrived with Louise and told us Kirsty's heart and breathing had stopped; the crash team were trying to resuscitate her.

Through that dreadful night we talked, we reminisced, we cried, we drank, we flopped, we waited and waited. Sue made soup, Louise stirred and Sue forced us all to eat something – Mother Earth as always! We were a group bonded together by love of Kirsty and the hope and despair that went with that love.

Steve called again at midnight with better news. Kirsty now had a forty-five percent chance of survival but the next twelve hours were critical. Phil and Louise left to go home. I stayed at Sue's and, though she gave me two sleeping tablets, I woke at 5 a.m. to phone Steve. By this time Kirsty had been moved to the Royal Manchester Children's Hospital and was on a life-support machine.

Saturday was surreal. I knew that the 90th celebration had to go on – Sue's mum Margaret is not going to be 90 again – but already the radio stations had started phoning me, asking if Kirsty was dead. There is always someone ready to spread bad news. I waited until just before 7 a.m. then called Paul Horrocks, the Editor of the *Manchester Evening News* and a loyal patron of our Appeal. It was vitally important to let Paul know the real situation.

Then, still early in the morning, I went to see Kirsty in Pendlebury. I expected to see her in bed surrounded by her family but Lynn, Steve, Zoe and Kim were all exhausted; they had been up all night and were now in the day room. As I entered the intensive care ward I could see Kirsty lying there. She looked so fragile, so incredibly poorly. I prayed that she would open her eyes and start cheating at cards as she normally did.

I went through with the birthday event – somehow. There were all these people screaming at the horse races or reacting to the singer, Cole Page, enjoying their food and wine. Not five percent of them were aware how forced were some of our smiles.

At the first opportunity I phoned David and Victoria Beckham and Mr Al Fayed and I have to confess that when I spoke to them I did not think Kirsty would make it. The Beckhams and Mr Al Fayed were in constant touch and David made me promise to let him know if she regained consciousness, as he wanted to speak to her as soon as he could.

That night, Kirsty opened her eyes. Sunday morning arrived and she regained consciousness.

It is hard to believe after the events of the previous two days that, when I told Kirsty that David Beckham wanted to speak to her, she beamed as I passed her the phone. There was a gentle nodding and quiet words. David said that he was very proud of her and if she continued to be a very brave girl he would send her the latest Real Madrid strip.

Kirsty on call after her relapse, in Wythenshawe Hospital, July 2005. (SM for MEN)

By then the world's press all knew that Kirsty was facing her biggest battle. Someone had leaked the news of David's phone call and it certainly wasn't me. Although David and Victoria had consistently supported us for many years, they had both kept their close relationship with Kirsty private. I phoned Victoria and asked her how she wanted me to respond. She told me she trusted me to say whatever I thought appropriate. Considering the media frenzy around the Beckhams and their status as celebrities, that trust meant an awful lot to me.

The news coverage was extensive and, as Kirsty slowly recovered, we kept everyone updated with accurate reports. The press hounded me for an up-to-date picture proving that Kirsty was alive and so, since I would not allow any photographers anywhere near her ward, the *Manchester Evening News* gave me a camera with which to prove that our little girl was on the road to recovery.

Life is fleeting and none of us knows for sure whether we will still be here in the next year or even in the next hour. In that sense we are all terminally ill but we tend to act as if this is something we do not know. Kirsty's hold on life is so slender that it should force us to face the reality, but the shock was no less great when we thought that we had lost her and Phil and I did not sleep soundly for many, many days.

It may be that by the time you read this book, the heart that has kept beating so much longer than anyone expected could have failed, but in the meantime Kirsty fights on and I believe that the £5m goal has helped her and given focus to that fight as well as helping so many others in the future.

I will leave the closing words for her father.

'After Kirsty's cardiac arrest her recuperation was, as always, at Francis House Children's Hospice and on this occasion, the privacy and the care was even more appreciated. The Hospice is a wonderful place. Children love being there and, because of

Kirsty recovers from her relapse. (SM for MEN)

that, it gives parents and siblings the time we need to relax and recharge our batteries.

'Kirsty has loved every minute of the last five years. We thought that she might get nervous at meeting famous people but she has taken everything in her stride and has not let one thing, or one person, faze her. Since the Appeal began she has met many people, famous and otherwise. Her first and favourite friend is David Beckham, her musical friend is Ronan Keating. As far as television goes, she adores *Coronation Street* and, although she loves all her patrons and especially Liz and Bill, her favourite is Richard Fleeshman.

'Lynn and I are proud of all our children; we have been blessed with three beautiful girls. We are obviously so proud that Kirsty will reach her target of £5 million. She has defied all the odds and long may she continue to do so. Kirsty is now looking forward to her Angel Ball party, where we will celebrate with all our family and friends.'

Reflections

Are there any superlatives left to describe Kirsty's profound existence? She has achieved more in her eleven years than most of us do in a full lifetime.

To lose Kirsty is incomprehensible. To lose Francis House is unthinkable.

When this Campaign began the financial situation looked like this:

Annual running costs	£1,500,000
Staff annual costs	£ 600,000

Support from the local Health Authorities	4%

Here we are six years later:

Annual running cost	£1,700,000
Annual Staff Costs	£1,000,000

Support from the local Health Authorities	1%

Kirsty has done more than any other individual to shine light upon the plight of Children's Hospices.

Kirsty's £5 million, by topping up the shortfalls, will give Francis House a well-deserved safety net but, with the running costs rising each year, and still no help from Central Government, the burden will still be great.

Philip will be remaining with Francis House to ensure that Kirsty's legacy continues. Please give him your support... 0800 097 1197.

As I retire from my fundraising years, my love and personal goals will continue for Kirsty. I would like to thank everyone who has contributed towards Kirsty's Appeal. Thanks also to my friends, who have stayed with me through all the in-between times.

I feel enormously privileged to have played a small part in an exceptional little girl's life: Kirsty.

OUR KIND OF PEOPLE

Patrons
Sue Johnston – Actress

Our first patron was Sue Johnston, of *The Royle Family*. She could hardly say no, she couldn't escape, she lives next door to me! Sue will always be our Royle and her commitment to the Appeal is total. She continuously champions our cause, is always on the lookout for raffle and auction prizes and cajoles other people to attend and support us.

Sue has become emotionally involved with the Howards as a family. There have been many times over the past years when Sue's words of encouragement have helped Lynn and Steve through horrendous predicaments.

Of course, if the Angel Ball ever clashed with a Liverpool game, no contest.

Kirsty with her Patron, Sue Johnston – and teddy bears. (SG)

Colin Lane – Times Newspaper Group

It is now five years since I met Colin and he is one hell of a guy. From the first meeting at Francis House, through the numerous ups and downs as we started the Appeal, he has given unstinting support. He is one of the funniest and most entertaining of people. His wicked sense of humour kicks in on some serious situations. It has been Colin's part to cajole newspapers to give us space and to liaise with TV companies for realistic deals.

Paul Horrocks – Editor *Manchester Evening News*

Paul has been an amazing patron; without him we would never have received the phenomenal amount of publicity. As editor of the *Manchester Evening News* he helped get the backing of big

Paul Horrocks, Patron and Editor of the Manchester Evening News, *presents a cheque from the MEN team who climbed Kilimanjaro – Angel Ball 2005. (MEN)*

businesses. For example, when Walt Disney wanted to do an advertising piece with the MEN, Paul chose us to be the beneficiaries of monies raised. He has donated prizes, he has bought tables for all events and he has more than fulfilled his promises. I think climbing Kilimanjaro says it all!

Dr Harold Riley – Artist
Dr Harold Riley was an obvious choice as he is respected worldwide. He has donated beautiful paintings which have raised thousands of pounds in our auctions. He has also personalized Christmas cards. Harold was a student of Lowry. His art works are sought after internationally and may be found hanging in the most famous galleries, basilicas and homes (including Kirsty's!).

Tracy Shaw – Actress
Tracy attended a couple of very important fundraising initiatives when she was starring in *Coronation Street* and, as an A1 celebrity, her photograph guaranteed national press. I wrote formally and asked her if would she become a patron and immediately, she gave a resounding YES.

Sally Lindsay – Actress
We first met Sally at a fundraising event at the White Lounge Altrincham. When she arrived she immediately achieved a special rapport with Kirsty. There was no celebrity edge, she thoroughly enjoyed herself taking hold of the reins for the evening and cajoling and generally bombarding people with enthusiasm. 'That's my kind of girl' and so, when we were asking for people to support the Southport Paul Yaffe ball, we invited Sally and it was there that I asked her to become a patron.

Samia Smith née Ghadie – Actress
Samia started attending events and even ran the Great Manchester Run before becoming a patron. *Coronation Street's* popularity is enormous and so of course are cast members. Samia plays Maria and she is as beautiful as a person as she is as an actress. She radiates sunshine wherever she goes and

Patron Shobna Gulati presents – at the 2005 Angel Ball.

she always responds positively to any requests that we make for her help.

Shobna Gulati – Actress
Shobna Gulati , famous for her roles in *Dinnerladies, Coronation Street* and now *Where the Heart Is* has really challenged herself whilst being our patron. She even survived the onslaught from Anne Robinson on *The Weakest Link*. Shobna's support spread through her family as her mum, president of the Inner Wheel, chose our appeal to receive the benefits from a wonderful luncheon where Shobna had persuaded 10 members of the cast to be there.

Russell Watson – Opera Singer
Russell Watson I have known personally for many years and have witnessed first hand his tremendous rise to fame. Having sold more albums than Madonna, his popularity was reaching its pinnacle when he sang at the opening ceremony of the Commonwealth Games. Following that sensational ceremony,

Russell was so moved by Kirsty that he decided to make a record especially for her, which he duly did. Russell also recently gave us the profits from his win on *The Two of Us*.

Kate Holland – Marketing at The Trafford Centre
Kate Holland is a very important person. She has been the decision maker for fundraising at the Trafford Centre from its inception. Kate is also important to me personally. She is a strong and wonderful woman and, when I finally got to meet her after years of begging letters, it was as if we had been friends forever. Kate has run for us, given 100% support on behalf of the Trafford Centre and she has also been 'gunged' for us. She is brilliant.

Mark Rix – MEN Media Sales
Mark is a Deputy Managing Director of the *Manchester Evening News*. We first met at a luncheon with Paul Horrocks. It was the first social fundraising event since my breast cancer and it was

Kirsty shows her Patron Mark Rix how to ride a bike, before his team sets off from Lands End to ride to John o' Groats. (MEN)

there that I implored them both to do whatever they could to get us to the end of the Appeal. Mark has cycled from Land's End to John O'Groats and he instigated the gruelling trip to Kilimanjaro. Mark is a strong and kind man.

Mr Mohamed Al Fayed – Harrods
Mr Al Fayed has been the largest single donor to Kirsty's Appeal, and his encouragement and enthusiasm have moved this Appeal towards our goal. Through Mr Al Fayed's friendship we have received donations from very high-profile celebrities. Harrods hampers have graced all our events and the generosity that you have read about is nothing compared to all the wonderful things that he has done for both the charity and the Howard family.

Paul Beck – Chief Executive L.B.M. Solutions
We have so many things to thank Paul for, not least the introduction to Freddie Flintoff. Paul, as the Chairman of Glenn Chapple and Freddie Flintoff's benefits, has included our appeal and raised vast amounts of money for us. He has

Patron Paul Beck at Lancashire Cricket Club. (LBM)

donated many fabulous prizes, always supported our events and usually buys at least two items in the auction.

Words from Patrons and Supporters
Mr Al Fayed
'I was deeply touched by Kirsty's plight after reading about her in a newspaper. I was determined to do something for her and went to Francis House to meet her and her family. As soon as we met I was completely bowled over by this little angel. Whenever I see her it makes me happy because she has such an engaging personality and bears her disability with such bravery that she inspires everyone around her.

'I will never forget the Christmas when Kirsty came to visit Santa's grotto at Harrods. She was dressed all in red and sat on Father Christmas's knee looking just like one of his little elves. All the customers and their children were captivated by her beaming smile. That was one of many visits that Kirsty and her family have made to the store. Soon after we met I brought the

Kirsty shows Patron Mohamed Al Fayed round Francis House, in 2003.
(MEN)

world's leading specialist in her condition from America to Britain to help. He was able to suggest treatments which stabilized the situation and improved the quality of Kirsty's life slightly. But there was nothing significant that he could achieve in the long term so we must continue to pray for a cure for this adorable little poppet.'

Liz Dawn – Coronation Street Actress
'Kirsty has the face of an Angel; her goodness shines through with every smile. Whenever I see Kirsty I am always amazed at her patience and eagerness to please. For someone so young to pull at the heartstrings by a look and a happy heart is such an inspiration to others. Kirsty's parents must be so proud of such a blessed daughter. I love to see the special bond between Susie Mathis and Kirsty. Whenever she appears at fundraising events she could be with other celebrities such as David Beckham or the Queen but she outshines them all, she is THE STAR!'

Actress Sue Johnston
'Susie Mathis is my friend and next door neighbour and had just started her project fundraising for a hospice with a little girl called Kirsty fronting the appeal. She said she was coming round to visit and would I meet her? My first impression on seeing her as she was then, four years old and very frail attached to this tank, was quite distressing but within seconds you realise that pity didn't come into it, she didn't ask for any. She was an ordinary, colourful, endearing, perceptive and amazing little girl. She loved coming into the garden and seeing all the animals we have here and they seemed to be very sensitive to her and adored her. She always calls me SueJohnston like one big name, never anything else. My son, like every man, fell totally in love with her and being rather a good cook, he once made her a spaghetti bolognese when she was staying over with us for the weekend. Now he has to cook it for her on a regular basis and it is called 'SueJohnstonssonsJoelsspaghettibolognese'.

'I have met many "stars" but I have never met anyone quite like Kirsty. She actually doesn't give a hoot who people are. She likes them or she doesn't like them, be they the Queen, David

Kirsty joins The Royle Family *and friends – left to right: Sue Johnston, Claire Sweeney, Ricky Tomlinson and Michael Stark. (MEN)*

Beckham or a porter at the hospital. She embraces them all or she gives them short shrift. She is her own person, she does not ask for sympathy, she has no self pity.

'I ran the Manchester Run for her, which I would not do for any other mortal person; my feet are still killing me 6 months later, but it was still worth it.

'When she comes to stay with us, the house lights up, everything changes, Kirsty rules. We do lots of girly things and she makes us all roar with laughter. She has a gift, a wonderful gift for life. There is something special about her existence and we are all better for knowing her.'

Freddie Flintoff, England cricket Captain
'When I met Kirsty at her Angel Ball I instantly knew I was in the company of someone very special – not just because of the millions of pounds she's helped raise for Francis House or because of her constant fight with illness, but because this

Cricketer Freddie Flintoff and Kirsty up close at Francis House, as Freddie pledges support from his benefit year, 2006. (MEN)

young girl had the ability to inspire a room of 500 people to do good and make a difference.

'Sportsmen, actors, businessmen – no matter who you are, two minutes in Kirsty's company and one big beaming smile and you're hooked – I was no different and, when given the tour from Kirsty of Francis House, meeting her friends and their parents, the wanting to get involved in this great cause was compounded and through my benefit year has given me the perfect opportunity to do so.

'To raise nearly five million pounds in five years is a tremendous effort for all those involved and has given children and parents alike much needed help.

'As for Kirsty, I'm sure your family are extremely proud of everything you've achieved and so should you be. You have a special place in my family's heart and thank you for the impact you've had on our lives.

'I look forward to attending many more Angel Balls,
'All our love

'Fred, Rachael, Holly and Corey '

xxxxxxxxxxx

Russ Vine – CheethamBellJWT – Advertising Agency

'CheethamBellJWT have been offering Francis House/The Kirsty Appeal their services as an advertising agency for five years now. Our role is to help Susie and the team use adverts and marketing activity in general to help raise funds.

'Over the years we've come up with all sorts of angles and ideas to try and eke a few more pence out of the public. It should be easy is stating the obvious, to simply say "This vital work carried out by Francis House is entirely dependent on contributions from the public and if everybody gave just a little bit, the respite of so many kids could be guaranteed".

'But it's not that easy. Because they are not the only charity and because, when a society moves as fast as the one we live in, stopping to give just a little can seem beyond most people.

'But that's where Kirsty comes in . . .

'Kirsty stops people, not just because she is adorable and cute or because her image tugs on your heart strings like a tonne weight. Kirsty stops people because, if she can do something to help, you sure as hell should be able to. Her bravery is beyond astounding, her smile in the face of adversity a lesson to us all. We've put all sorts of famous people in all sorts of ads before but Kirsty's by far the biggest star we've ever worked with!'

Chris Tarrant – TV Presenter

'My memories of Kirsty and her lovely family are from the day that I sat next to her at the Pride of Britain Awards. She had bits of tubing sticking out from all over her dear little face and a giant oxygen tank had to follow her everywhere she went, including when she went up on to the stage to get her award. But she couldn't have been more cheerful; she simply radiated happiness and joy to everybody she met, everybody who saw her. She is a wonderful inspiration to all of us. Her attitude is amazing and her courage is extraordinary.

'I think I was the first person on radio in this country to play the beautiful song dedicated to her by Russell Watson, and it's quite impossible to hear that haunting tune without seeing the image of Kirsty's beautiful, smiling face.

'She is a remarkable little girl.'

Chris Tarrant. (DM)

Paul Horrocks – Editor *MEN* – Patron

'Kirsty will love this book about her – and so she should because for a child of such tender years, she has already achieved more that many will do in their whole lifetime. Celebrities, politicians, football superstars and even the Queen at the Commonwealth Games, she has greeted them all with not a moment's hesitation. I have heard people say that she has been used and that it has put added pressure on a sick child. Anyone who has ever met Kirsty will know that it is not true. She loves the limelight, she has a special glow whenever she is centre stage – and anyone who looks into those deep blue eyes is captivated

'I first met Kirsty over lunch at Francis House. She took me on a guided tour of the Hospice. As I hauled her oxygen tank, she made me realise what a special place it is. Her face beamed with excitement as we entered her favourite room, the lighthouse it is. Over lunch around the table with her mum and dad, I encouraged her to eat her jacket potato with cheese but she only nibbled her food. Kirsty engages you with a smile, and then she's off, her attention turned to yet another visitor.

'At the Angel Ball she cuddled on my knee for a photograph in her red fairy outfit, and every time I look at that picture on my desk at home, I know why Kirsty's Appeal is so important for lots of children, and why she will always have a special place in my heart – and the affections of everyone at the *Manchester Evening News.* '

Richard Bowden – Sterling Events – and Kirsty's Number 1 Boyfriend!

'I'd like to tell you about the first time Kirsty and I really bonded, at a small gathering at the Radisson Hotel a few years back. I was playing music when Kirsty arrived, she walked straight up to me and with lots of confidence asked, "Will you play Ronan Keating please". I played her request, while she stood next to me giving me the thumbs up and singing to every word. Kirsty kept me company that night and since then the Ronan Keating song *When you Say Nothing at All* has been our song.

'We met again a few weeks later when Kirsty introduced me to her family as her boyfriend, at which I felt honoured; all the celebrity friends she has made and Kirsty liked me.

'Getting to know Kirsty better by now I found out her dislikes – other women! If another woman comes anywhere near me she becomes very protective. I've never seen Kirsty without a big smile on her face; even if she is tired, she is always happy. That has to be the thing I admire most about her.'

Rachael Bletchly – Chief Feature Writer *Sunday People*

'I first met Kirsty at Francis House at Easter 2000. *The People* had decided to back her Appeal and I was sent to meet "the girl with the mile-wide smile" who had already captured our readers' hearts. My first impression was of a pair of big blue eyes... and then those tiny fingers with this sparkly nail varnish dipping in and out of a bag of Prawn Cocktail Crisps!

'She looked so tiny but she had more inner strength than ANY of the world leaders, politicians or sporting giants I have interviewed. Ten months later, I accompanied Kirsty to Downing Street to meet Prime Minister, Tony Blair – and I knew that feeling was right. Unfazed by the grand surroundings – "your house is posh, isn't it?" she told Cherie – she simply tucked into the PM's biscuits and played with his baby son, Leo.

'But, Mr Blair seemed awestruck as he watched Kirsty enjoying life and defying the doctors. Planting a kiss on her head, it was clear he could sense Kirsty's incredible fighting spirit too.

'Kirsty has met a lot of famous people since then – The Queen, David Beckham and countless pop stars. And standing beside Kirsty, every one of them seems more human and more ordinary.

'For Kirsty touches something inside ALL of us and teaches us how precious life is.

'And no matter how many millions this incredible child raises for her Hospice THAT is Kirsty's lasting legacy. '

Martin Spaven – Chief Photographer, *The People*
'Looking back over the thousands of frames that I have taken of her and seeing how she has grown, makes me think of my own three girls

'Over the past four years, I have captured many milestone moments in Kirsty's incredible life. I have visited her in hospital when she has looked so pale and tired it made my heart miss a beat... but, she could still raise a smile. And I have seen her tearing around like a racing driver in her wheelchair and lighting up with joy when she met the "real" Santa at Harrods.

'The amazing thing about Kirsty is that no matter what problems are on YOUR mind, thirty seconds in her company is enough to make you forget them all. Her throaty laugh and cheeky jokes (often a bit TOO cheeky for such an angel-faced youngster!) are like a tonic.

'It has been a privilege for me to capture the birthdays, Christmases, Easters and Summer Holidays that doctors never thought she would live to see.

'It has been a joy to snap her meeting her hero Becks, pop heartthrob Ronan Keating and seeing her get her hair blow-dried by chief admirer – Mohammed Al Fayed.

'But I think my favourite memory has to be our trip to Disneyland Paris two years ago. Kirsty had never been abroad before – and nearly missed the dream trip because she was back in hospital the week before with a chest infection. But she was desperate to meet Mickey and she summoned all her strength for the trip. When we arrived in Paris, Mum got Kirsty dressed in her new Minnie Mouse outfit, Dad Steve carried her into the magic kingdom and Kirsty's eyes lit up at her first sight of Sleeping Beauty's Castle.

' "Do you think I can take a quick photo of Kirsty?" I asked.

' "Put me down Dad," she said. "Where do you want me then Martin?"

'Now THAT is star quality.'

Samia Smith née Ghadie – Patron

'The first time that I met Kirsty was at the Paul Yaffe Ball in Southport and my first impression was quite tough for me as I felt as if I wanted to cry. But within five minutes her courage makes you forget she is poorly at all and her brilliant personality shines. That night was so special. I remember vividly Kirsty being presented with a beautiful doll from Sandra who organised the event and Kirsty made my heart sink when she named her doll after her two sisters, Kim and Zoe. As we enjoyed our meal, she enjoyed chips and beans and fed her doll.

'Since then I have run the Great Manchester Run on two occasions and thoroughly enjoyed this special event. Kirsty amazed me how she charged around at enormous speed in her wheelchair. . . .

'My very special memory of closeness with such a unique little girl was at the launch of Spiderman at the Trafford Centre when after the ceremony had ended she held her little arms up for me to hold her and clasped me really really tight and told me she could not believe that so many people had come to see her.

'Kirsty is a truly amazing, precious little angel and anyone that meets her, can't help but fall in love instantly, as I did.'

Russell Watson – Patron

'In the last five years I have had the opportunity to meet some incredible people, from movie stars to famous sports personalities, many of whom excel beyond the boundaries of what we would consider to be normal. Some of them have left long-lasting impressions on me. Others, I have viewed carefully and learnt from. Some have inspired me, some have heartened me and some have impressed me. There is one person however who stands above and beyond these in my memory. She is not a Pope, a President, or a Pop Star. She is not a sports person or a movie star. She is a seven-year-old girl by the name of Kirsty Howard: a tiny little thing with a pale complexion, fragile in appearance but with an inner strength that transcends her appearance. I remember just before I met Kirsty thinking first of all "What will I say to this little girl who had been born with her internal organs back to front and had been given little chance of survival by doctors?". Boy, was I in for a surprise? She can talk the hind legs off a donkey! Very funny, very talkative, and very smart for a child of her age. She has a wicked sense of humour and because of her personality you find it very easy to forget that she actually has a problem. One of the funniest of my encounters with Kirsty was after having been told by Susie Mathis that Kirsty had taken quite a shine to me. Susie was joking with Kirsty saying that I was her boyfriend. Kirsty responded sharply, quickly, and abruptly "I don't think so Susie!! Go away, leave him alone he's mine!". Even funnier when I introduced my fiancée Roxana to Kirsty. Kirsty would have nothing whatsoever to do with her. She stared her up and down and then turned away. We all had a good laugh about it afterwards. Kirsty always insists on a kiss when I see her and I am told that she is usually quite conservative with these. I guess what I am trying to say is bravery, strength and determination from within seldom comes in such small packages. Kirsty Howard is a one-off. She's battled against the odds and won hands down. Long may that continue and long may she continue to inspire people as she's inspired me.'

Dr Harold Riley – Patron
'I first met little Kirsty in the back garden of the house where she lived in Manchester. She was having her photograph taken and the photographers fussed around her, busily arranging various positions and poses.

*Kirsty looks at her special Christmas card, created by Patron
Dr Harold Riley. (MEN)*

'She conducted herself like someone who was totally oblivious of anything except what they wanted her to do. She was not an ordinary little girl because she had a glowing charisma.

'After a while she had her photograph taken with me, her soft liquid eyes held mine for a moment and she softly laid her cheek against mine; she had won me over as she has thousands of people.

'Not long afterwards she sat for me whilst I made a portrait drawing of her, a little girl on one hand and an amazing and tireless worker on the other; thousands of children in the future will benefit from her ceaseless efforts and her star will shine forever.

'Sometimes in life we witness something that stays forever in our minds, Kirsty will stay forever in my heart.'

Mark Rix– Patron
'Imagine standing on the summit of Mount Kilimanjaro in Tanzania, the highest point on the African continent and the world's highest free-standing mountain.

'The curvature of the planet is visible 360 degrees along the horizon of the clouds some 10,000 ft below you and your body struggles for breath with only 40% oxygen available compared to sea level, whilst sub-zero temperatures sap your energy with a wind chill that cuts through your specialist mountain clothing like a hot knife through butter and after a final overnight gruelling hike from base camp lasting 13 hours, you ask yourself...... was the past five days on this mountain worth it?

'We generally take our good health and fitness for granted, yet when your body is taken to extremes, it is perhaps possible to understand a fraction of the hardship suffered and determination to conquer it that epitomises Kirsty Howard and all the wonderful children her fantastic appeal has helped and aims to provide for in perpetuity at Francis House Children's Hospice.

'The decision to organise an expedition to climb Mount Kilimanjaro was made on the journey back from John O'Groats in September 2004 after cycling there from Land's End over ten days. Our team of five cyclists and our support vehicle driver had covered 976 miles in ten days and raised around £15,000 for Kirsty's Appeal. We realised that we could do better and set ourselves a target for the following summer of £50,000.

'The eight months or so training for the cycle ride was great preparation for a further eight months conditioning to get up Kilimanjaro. We decided that this was one way to help Kirsty (and Susie, Phil and all the team at the Appeal) climb her own mountain – to raise five million pounds and secure the future of Francis House.

'Our team was drawn from all walks of life and all were touched by Kirsty's bravery, stamina and wonderful personality, the inimitable drive and support of Susie and fundamentally, the wish to help.

'Between the following people, including both the Land's End to John O'Groats cycle ride and the Kilimanjaro climb, Philip Tonge, Ian Marshall, Paul O'Halloran, Ron Bent, Dave Healey, Hervey Magnall, David Rix, Paul Horrocks, Phil Davenport and myself, we raised £137,000 and will be forever proud that this in some way contributed towards the magnificent achievement of Kirsty's Appeal in reaching the target of £5 million.

'When Kirsty put her arms around me and gave me a kiss at the Angel Ball in 2005 and said thank you, the endless hours of cycling, climbing, hiking, travelling, training and fundraising paled into insignificance.

'This kid melts your heart.'

Sally Lindsay – Patron

'I have many happy memories of this special little girl, but she possesses a quality which I find most commendable; an immense ability to override her disability and enjoy life to the full.

'The most poignant memory of this comes from when I attended one of the many events to raise money for "The Kirsty Appeal". It was a very star-studded, glitzy event and

Patron Sally Lindsay joins Kirsty and fellow Patron Samia Smith at the Paul Yaffe Ball in Southport, November 2003. (YFA)

everybody was looking their best. Kirsty was the belle of the ball, but it still was very obvious to me that she was growing into a young lady, her dress was a little more grown-up and her shoes a bit more pointed, but more importantly she had been allowed to wear lip gloss!!

'After the auction, and after her meeting a million people, she asked me if I'd go to the loo with her and, like all young ladies she had me take her handbag with us. When we were washing our hands she asked me to pass her lip gloss, I said she could have a go at mine, but she said "No thank you I have a special one.". I took hers out of her bag . . . . . . it was purple, like her lips "That's my colour, you see." she said joyfully.

'It took every fibre in me not to burst into tears . . . . . . Whenever I am feeling sorry for myself, because of Kirsty, I remember the colour of my lipstick. '

Kate Holland – Patron – The Trafford Centre

'When the Centre opened in September 1998, fountains situated throughout were used for people to throw their loose change and it was decided that this money should be distributed to local charities. From research carried out in the Centre, local hospitals and hospices, and children's hospices in particular were recognised as the preferred type of charities to benefit from fund-raising.

'Charities that fitted these criteria were approached and invited to apply for funding. During the first five years 12 different local charities benefited each year from approximately £25,000 from the Centre. In the first year, this included Francis House Children's Hospice. Susie Mathis, fund-raiser for the Kirsty Appeal, made numerous approaches to me regarding the funding from the fountains and in 2002 The Kirsty Appeal was selected to benefit from the Centre. Susie's enthusiasm, energy and determination enthused me and made me want to support this incredible, brave girl in securing the future of this wonderful hospice.

'Between 2002 and July '06, £119,061.54 has been raised for the Appeal via the Centre. Retailers and staff have been very supportive of the cause and many individuals have got involved with their own sponsored events for Kirsty.

*Patron Kate Holland is on the receiving end of the
Trafford Centre's gunging. (TC)*

'Kirsty has been to the Centre many times to launch new
fund-raising campaigns. One event in particular, which raised
just over £34,000, was a Spiderman Campaign whereby
Spiderman badges were sold at stores and restaurants
throughout the Centre. Kirsty attended the launch with a
number of celebrities and Simon Gregson *aka* Steve McDonald
from *Coronation Street* assumed a Spiderman costume and
abseiled down the huge big screen much to the amazement of
our customers.

'My most special memory was when Kirsty celebrated her
10th birthday at the Trafford Centre and Richard Fleeshman
sang *Happy Birthday* to her. Kirsty had only recently been

seriously ill in hospital, and to see her that day in high spirits to celebrate her birthday was truly memorable and emotional.

'It was a great honour that Susie Mathis asked me to be a patron of this charity in 2004. I felt a huge sense of pride to be involved with such a wonderful charity and very privileged.

'Kirsty means so much to all of us here at the Centre. Her witty charm and personable attributes, along with her incredible bravery, has warmed all of our hearts.

'Susie Mathis and the team should also be recognised for their amazing work. Susie's dogged determination has meant that this £5 million project is now almost complete. She has been the underpin of this hugely successful campaign and she is greatly admired by us.'

Bill Tarmey – Actor
'Meeting brave and beautiful little Kirsty Howard is a truly memorable experience for anyone fortunate enough to do so. It certainly was for me.

Coronation Street's *Bill Tarmey has Kirsty's lipstick on his forehead!* *(MEN)*

'About six years ago, I was patiently awaiting my turn at the anti-coagulant clinic at Wythenshawe Hospital when there was a rather unusual "clunking" and I looked up to see a tiny, tiny little girl with great big eyes who was attached to an oxygen bottle and tubes coming out of her nose. The oxygen was being wheeled around by her mother (hence the clunking) and she was holding the hand of one of her older sisters. Before long, this vibrant little girl had captivated everyone; she was like a ray of sunshine.

'I asked her mother about the necessity for the oxygen bottle and when she told of little Kirsty's rare and terminal heart condition, I had difficulty in holding back the tears. Mrs Howard explained how they were hoping to find someone to assist with fundraising, to help not only Kirsty, but to help other terminally ill children. My immediate advice was that she should contact the dynamic Susie Mathis.

'Kirsty was sitting on my knee when I was called in for my appointment, I gave her and her sister a little kiss and said that this was a really special day for me, as not only was it my birthday, but I had met a unique and special little girl.

'As I was leaving the hospital, I heard my name being shouted, and when I turned around, Kirsty, her sister (and mother lugging the oxygen bottle) came running up to me and handed me a birthday card, which they had hurriedly been and bought. I was absolutely thrilled.

'Kirsty amazed and inspired me at that first meeting and has continued to do so ever since.'

Richard Fleeshman – Actor and Singer

'I'd heard about Kirsty and sometimes seen her on TV and in newspapers but didn't actually meet her until I was invited to sing at her 8th birthday party.

She came up on stage and I sang *You Look Wonderful Tonight*. She did, she wore a gorgeous red dress and looked like a princess.

'I bought her a little soft toy and thought she'd think I was a bit stupid getting her that but she loved it and told Susie Mathis it was her favourite present. It made me feel very special (but maybe she said that to all her boyfriends!).

Kirsty with Coronation Street's *Richard Fleeshman at the Trafford Centre. (MEN)*

'That's one of the amazing things about Kirsty; she manages to make people feel very special and she doesn't realise just how special *she* is.

'Of course, we all feel sad that she's having to cope with so much but she still makes me smile every time we meet AND much more importantly, SHE's always smiling.

'When I took part in Soapstar Superstar last January and I was asked which Charity I would like any money to go to, I didn't hesitate, it had to be the Kirsty Appeal.

'I didn't know then that I'd be able to present Kirsty with a cheque for £200,000; that felt great and she was thrilled to bits that she was reaching her goal with the help of so many friends.

'Kirsty presented me with a beautiful painting of herself and it takes pride of place on our living room wall at home.

'Every time I look at her face she makes me smile and always will.'

Shobna Gulati – Patron
'When l first met Kirsty, l was moved by her charm, charisma and determination.

128

'Her little face and sweet smile conceals "One Tough Cookie".

'She made me stop... and think about what it is to live life... I have made a conscious thought to choose to live from moment to moment as if every precious second is my last, also knowing that I have the responsibility of leaving a legacy to help others lead a better life.

'She is my figurehead, my role model. Knowing her has inspired me and many, to give a chance of living life however tenuous but so valuable to those terminally ill children at Francis House.

'I recommend The Kirsty Way... to everyone.'

Zoe Howard, sister

'When I was nine years old my mum and dad asked my sister and I to go downstairs as they had some important news. Mum, Dad, my godmother Linda, Aunty Denise and Uncle Keith were there. We both knew there was something wrong. They told us that Kirsty had only been given 3-6 weeks to live. We ran up to Kirsty's bedroom and grabbed a teddy bear each. I picked her favourite, Barney. We were going to keep them to remember her.

'Anyway, 3–6 weeks had passed and she was still with us. It was like a miracle. I'm her elder sister and she tends to look up to me. We do the typical girly things that sisters do. From then we treated every minute as though it was our last and we spend as much time together and make it as much fun as possible.

'Kirsty is a cheeky little monkey at times, some of the stuff that she comes out with has people rolling about laughing.

'I do have to admit at times, I find it really difficult coping with the situation, but then I think to myself, what's the point in getting all upset because she is still with us, isn't she?'

Kim Howard, sister

'When I heard my baby sister only had 3-6 weeks to live, it didn't register. I remember saying to everyone "Why can't it be me?" She's only a baby, this shouldn't happen to a baby. My family and I thought our world was going to end, but luckily enough it didn't.

'The Angel Balls are amazing. It's fantastic that celebrities take time out of their busy lives to appear at the balls. I can remember the first time, it was out of this world – like a dream or a fantasy. I was so excited to be around my idols and one of my biggest and bravest idols is Kirsty.

'I love it at Francis House because nobody judges you. I hate it when people judge disabled people just for the simple fact that they are disabled. They seem to forget that everyone has feelings and may find certain things offensive. Kirsty is a huge inspiration to any disabled child because if she can cope then I'm sure any other person can do the same.'

THE FINAL WORDS ARE KIRSTY'S

Kirsty Howard has captured hearts across the nation and the world.

Her appeal lies in the combination of her condition and her courage, her tender years and her maturity, her physical frailty and her indomitable spirit.

Her Appeal has succeeded through the efforts of many people – family, friends, stars and celebrities, but above all, the sheer force of her personality.

In this celebration of her life, let Kirsty have the last words:

on the Angel Balls
'I like the Angel Balls because all my boyfriends will be there and we can raise a lot more money for the Appeal.'

'Before the ball I get to choose what type of dress I want and what colour. My favourite dress is my red one. Before the ball I go and get my hair done at Tony's; Tony is funny, he always asks who's going to be there.'

'Don't know who I have loved most as there are so many people who have been special.'

on the cruise
'The best bit of the cruise was when we stopped off at Corsica because I jumped the waves with Phil and Alex for the first time in my life.'

'The ship was big, the food was nice, loads to choose from, I ate a lot there – that's the main thing. I was having too much fun. I jumped the waves for the first time in Corsica. I wanted to jump the waves because my sisters were doing it. But then, my lead broke and Alex mended it The sea was fun. Alex and Phil chased my mum and she didn't want to go into the sea and she fell so she was already wet. That was funny. We buried Zoe first and then Alex buried me in the sand.'

on her hero, David Beckham

'David is special because he is kind and caring towards me.

'When Zoe passed her exams & David said "I didn't pass my exams – it's a good job I can kick a football" This story makes me laugh.

'Always special about David Beckham – liked walking out on the pitch when he was playing Greece. It was very exciting. I fancied him at the time and it made it very special – he will always be special to me.'

on the Commonwealth Games

'The games were a bit scary because there were so many people there. I was worried about the baton because I wasn't sure if I could carry it but luckily David was there to help me.

'We went out and waited for David to come round with the baton, we walked up to give it to the Queen. I waited with my arms wide open to give him a big hug.'

on the Great Manchester Runs

'I like the Great Manchester Run as I am always Number 1.'

A kiss for David Beckham at the Lowry Hotel in 2005. (CG MEN)

on Blackpool Lights

'I'd just got out of hospital that day and I went to Blackpool to turn on the lights with Ronan Keating. I thought he was gorgeous.'

on The Appeal

'Why I wanted to do the Appeal? To help keep Francis House open for all the children. It's exciting. I like the jacuzzi because it's nice and relaxing. The carers are funny. I like the computer room. I like to play with the music – I like the piano best. The hospice is better than the hospital because the food is better. Dean's a good cook.'

on Mr Al Fayed

'I think Mr Al Fayed is a great man to be with because he is always smiling.'

LEFT: Sir Alex Ferguson shows Kirsty how to golf at Man United's training ground while RIGHT: Kirsty peeps round rugby giant Jonah Lumo. (Both MEN)

in answer to some questions:

'Can you think of the funniest thing you have done or the things you have laughed at most'
'I can't because I laugh every day of my life'

'How does it make you feel to have raised £5 million?'
'It makes me feel so proud of myself.'

'What is the Hospice like?'
'The hospice is a great place to be because there is a lot to do and you can make new friends nearly every time you go in. The parents get a rest and they can stay in too and their brothers and sisters can stay if they have any brothers and sisters.'

Kirsty meets the Chuckle Brothers at the Opera House, Manchester. (LB)

ABOVE; Davina McColl shares a girly moment with Kirsty at the launch of the Swedish jewellery exhibition at Harrods in August 2004, and BELOW: Gloria Hunniford joins them with the proprietor. (Both HPO)

ABOVE: Man on the moon Neil Armstrong meets Kirsty at Tatton Park, September 2003, and BELOW: two years later, Coronation Street *veteran William Roach 'raises brass' for Kirsty at Bridgewater Hall, Manchester in June 2005. (Both MEN)*

ABOVE: Louise Blenkharn registers shocked delight at reaching £4 million while BELOW: Phil promotes Spiderman badges – all in 2004. (Both MEN)

ACKNOWLEDGEMENTS

My thanks go to, in alphabetical order:

Action Images Limited, Anthony James Hair, Avalon Group Limited, Alyson Jones, B.B.C Sports Personality of the Year, Bees Knees Limousines, Bernard Wood, Bird Consultancy, Breville, British Airways, Centre Parcs, Champion, Cheetham Bell JWT Limited, Cheshire Building Society, Coronation Street, Daily Mirror, Daily Telegraph, David & Jan Artingstall, David & Victoria Beckham, Design Karma, Drivetime Ltd, Esure.com, Express Newspaper Group, Football Association Official Photo Library, Freeth Cartwright LLP Solicitors, Gate Films, Gavin Smith at Hello Magazine, G Mex, Harrods Charitable Trust, H.S.L. Entertainment, Island Cruises, John Jeffay MEN, John & Martin at Hovington Limited, Joynes – Pike Group Ltd, Jon & Lin of John Pimblett & Sons Ltd, Kendals – House of Fraser, Lavelle Designs, L.B.M. Solutions, Lynn & Steve Howard, Lisa Escasany & Harrods, Lucy Lockett Ltd, Martin Spaven, Mahood Marquees, Manchester City Council, Manchester City Football Club, Manchester Evening News, Manchester United Football Club, Mike & Jan at Solway Exhibition Centre, Mountrose Limited, Nova International, Perry Hughes, Planet Mobile, Photographers & Picture Desk at M.E.N., (Emma Williams, Mark Waugh, Paul Simpson, Howard Walker, Chris Gleave, Richard Kendal), S.J.M.Concerts, Spex Opticians, Stratstones Saab Manchester, The People, The Royal Bank of Scotland, Times Newspaper Group, Trafford Centre, Yaffe Fusion Art, and every single person who has helped us achieve Kirsty's goal.

Key to caption credits

AIL	Action Images Ltd
CB JWT	Cheetham Bell JWT
CG MEN	Chris Gleave, *Manchester Evening News*
DM	*Daily Mirror*
DT	*Daily Telegraph*
HPO	Harrods Press Office
HR	Dr Harold Riley
LB	Louise Blenkharn
LBM	L.B.M.
MEN	*Manchester Evening News*
MH	Mark Hendley
MS P	Martin Spaven – *People*
NI	Nova International
PM CB JWT	Paul Moffat – Cheetham Bell JWT
RK	BBC PO Richard Kendal, BBC Press Office
SG	Smiles Gavers
SM for MEN	Susie Mathis for *Manchester Evening News*
TC	Trafford Centre
TD	Trish Davies
YFA	Yaffe Fusion Art

Susie Mathis was born in London and spent her early years at a stage school in Northampton, leaving aged 13 to join the local repertory theatre. She then sang and danced in musicals and productions in the West End and toured.

In 1967, along with two former school friends, Susie formed The Paper Dolls pop group and in 1968 the girls achieved great success with a massive hit *Something Here, Here in My Heart*. Then followed appearances on *Top of the Pops, Morecambe and Wise, The Two Ronnies*.

Susie continued to record, appearing on *Top of the Pops* under many guises, including Tiger Sue, The Madisons and Colorado. She then re-formed the Dolls, both touring and cabaret. Susie has either appeared or presented on T O T P's over four decades.

In 1979 Susie joined Piccadilly Radio and by 1981 became Independent Radio's first daytime presenter. Her subsequent success led to her prestigious Sony Radio Awards for 'Personality of the Year' in both 1985 and 1989.

Susie has contributed to many deserving causes and charities since 1981 and, although brought up in showbiz, she says the most rewarding part of her life has been with Kirsty.

NON-FICTION

No Big Deal about Becky Measures, with Simon Towers
'My breasts or my life' – beating cancer before it happens

'A testament to the human spirit'
Tessa Cunningham, Daily Mail

Becky Measures' forbear died in 1834 – of breast cancer. Her mother, Wendy, found the family tree blighted from generation to generation – and was the first to choose a preventative double mastectomy. Now Becky, 24, vivacious, blonde, a radio presenter, has done exactly the same and claims: 'It's no big deal'. This is Becky's story – from childhood, through her mother's trauma, her teenage years and her decision to take the battle to the big C.

Medavia Publishing
an imprint of Boltneck Publications of Bristol

Medavia is a major media agency and Medavia Publishing brings people in the present and facts about the past into print.